S0-DTD-464

Canadian Health Coalition
Coalition canadienne de la santé
2841 Riverside Dr., Ottawa, Ont. K1V 8X7

Dear Pauline,

Looking forward to working together on the CHC Board.

Regards,

Mike

Ill-Health Canada:

Putting food and drug company profits ahead of safety

by
Michael McBane

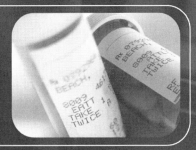

Canadian Centre for Policy Alternatives

Ill-Health Canada

Promoting Food and Drug Company
Profits Instead of Safety

By Michael McBane

Copyright 2005
All rights reserved. No part of this book may
be reproduced or transmitted in any form or by
any means, electronic or mechanical, including
photocopying, or by any information storage or
retrieval system, without permission in writing
from the publishers or the author.

Library and Archives Canada Cataloguing in
Publication

McBane, Michael
Ill-health Canada : promoting food and drug
company profits instead of safety / by Michael
McBane.

Includes bibliographical references.
ISBN 0-88627-405-2

1. Public health laws--Canada. 2. Public health
--Canada. 3. Canada.Health Canada. 4. Medical
policy--Canada. 5. Food law and legislation--Canada.
6. Drugs--Law and legislation--Canada. I. Canadian
Centre for Policy Alternatives. II. Title.

KE3575.M32 2005   344.7104   C2005-900053-8
KF3775.M32 2005

Cover design: Studio 2 (studio2@rogers.com)
Page layout: Tim Scarth

Printed and bound in Canada

Published by Canadian Centre for Policy Alternatives
410-75 Albert Street, Ottawa, ON K1P 5E7
tel: 613-563-1341 fax: 613-233-1458
email: ccpa@policyalternatives.ca
http://www.policyalternatives.ca

ACKNOWLEDGEMENT

This document was prepared by Michael McBane for the Canadian Health Coalition. It benefited from extensive comments provided by university scientists and researchers, federal government regulators, and public health guardians in Canada, England, and the United States.

DEDICATION

To the memory of the blood-injured and all who lost their lives because of the massive abdication of regulatory authority in Canada.

To the few courageous guardians at Health Canada – past and present – who follow their conscience, at great personal cost, and refuse to abandon their duty of care.

To the memory of Nicholas Regush, writer and journalist, 1946–2004. He exposed the heart of the matter.

ABOUT THE AUTHOR

Michael McBane is the National Coordinator of the Canadian Health Coalition, a public interest advocacy organization based in Ottawa (www.medicare.ca). For the past ten years he has been organizing resistance to the corporate virus infecting senior Health Canada managers in the Health Products and Food Branch.

Words of Wisdom

Words wreak havoc when they find a name for what had up to then been lived namelessly.

> – **Jean-Paul Sartre**, *L'idiot de la famille*, 1971

Societies need both commercial and guardian work...The two types are prone to corruption if they stray across either their functional or moral barriers.

> – **Jane Jacobs**, *Systems of Survival*, 1992

The relationship between a regulator and the regulated...must never become one in which the regulator loses sight of the principle that it regulates only in the public interest and not in the interest of the regulated.

> – **Justice Horace Krever**, *Commission of Inquiry on the Blood System in Canada*, 1996

Industry can't be regulated by government – and for environmental and health reasons they must be – if that government is in bed with them.

> – **_Globe & Mail_** editorial following the Westray
> Mine disaster, Dec. 2, 1997

Science is not bad, but there is bad science. Genetic engineering is bad science working with big business for quick profit against the public good.

> – **Mae-Wan Ho**, _Genetic engineering: Dream or
> Nightmare?_ 1998

To reassure us, they lie to us, and then treat us as idiots by insisting on things we all know are untrue. Not only does this prevent a reasonable debate from taking place, but it also creates a very unhealthy relationship between citizens and their elected representatives.

> – **John Ralston Saul**, "Health Care at the End of
> the Twentieth Century," 1999

The Panel identified...serious concerns about the undermining of the scientific basis for risk regulation in Canada due to... the conflict of interest created by giving to regulatory agencies the mandates both to promote the development of agricultural technologies and to regulate it.

> – **Royal Society of Canada**, _Expert Panel Report
> on the Future of Food Biotechnology_, 2001

In order to "stop breast cancer before it starts"...we need urgently to establish a different basis for regulatory practices.

> – **Laura Potts**, _Lies, Damn Lies and Public
> Protection: Corporate Responsibility and Breast
> Cancer Activism_, 2000.

Table of Contents

5   Open Letter to the Prime Minister
9   Summary
13 Recommendations
15 Introduction and Background

27 **1** Why Get Rid of the *Food & Drugs Act*?
33 **2** "Smart" Regulation or Safe Regulation?
37 **3** Krever and the Auditor-General on Legislative Change
41 **4** Changes to Strengthen and Renew?
47 **5** Risk Assessment
57 **6** General Safety Requirement
61 **7** Transparency of the Review Process
69 **8** Review of Novel (Genetically Modified) Food
77 **9** Direct-to-Consumer Drug Advertising
79 Notes on Key Terms
89 Appendix **1**
       10 Myths on Direct-to-Consumer Drug Advertising
95 Appendix **2**
       The Precautionary Principle (RSC Expert Panel)

119 40 Questions for Health Canada
125 References

Open Letter to the Prime Minister

Dear Prime Minister Paul Martin:

We are writing to express our deep concern with your government's proposal to replace Canada's *Food & Drugs Act* with a new health protection legislative regime. We have noted a series of changes announced by your new government that reflect the commitment to building a "21st century economy." A key element appears to be the re-design of the federal approach to health and safety regulation in order to create an "advantage" for industry by means of weaker safety standards.

Of particular concern are Health Canada's proposals to: a) abandon the Precautionary Principle to a narrow risk-benefit regime; b) shift the burden of proof from industry to the public: products to be presumed safe unless harm is proven; c) speed up drug approvals; and d) allow direct-to-consumer advertising of prescription drugs. If the government abdicates its health protection duty of care, Canada's health care system will not be able to cope with the negative health outcomes. The negative effects of these proposed regulatory changes would also be felt throughout the international community.

Societies need both commercial and guardian functions. But these two types of work are contradictory and are prone to corruption if they stray across either their moral or functional barriers. When the governments in Canada mix trade and industry objectives – like deregulation, self-regulation and privatization – into health protection functions, people are killed.

These are the painful lessons from the tainted blood disaster, drinking water contamination, adverse drug reactions, and deadly pathogens in food. Canada has not learned from the Mad Cow crisis in the U.K. that food safety and food promotion functions must not be housed within the same government agency. The federal regulator may have helped the Canadian beef industry economically in the short term by not adopting precautionary measures to stem the spread of Mad Cow disease. In the longer run, however, this lack of attention to safety will cost the industry much more.

The purpose of health protection legislation is to safeguard health and safety, not trade and investment. Government can't regulate to protect health and the environment – as the laws of Canada currently require – if it is in bed with the industries it regulates.

A health and safety regulatory agency that puts industry self-regulation for profit ("smart regulation") ahead of protecting public health is not moral, wise, or legal. Similarly, direct-to-consumer advertising of prescription drugs has only one aim: to promote product sales. Why would the federal government knowingly introduce a policy expected to undermine the sustainability of its health care services?

What kind of society builds a "21st Century economy" by exposing those least able to defend themselves – children and future generations – to uncontrollable hazards and unknown risk?

This is not the kind of Canada Canadians want. This is not the kind of Canada the world wants. This policy will not only put Canadians at risk, it will destroy Canada's international reputation. The end result will be to brand Canadian products as "dangerous."

We therefore urge you to instruct your Minister of Health to do the following:

1   Adopt the Precautionary Principle as the basis for a broad, transparent, and independent assessment of risk to

protect those least able to defend themselves from health hazards – especially children and future generations.

2 Terminate the "Health Protection Legislative Renewal" and uphold the "duty of care" in the current *Food & Drugs Act*.

3 Restore the burden of proof on industry to demonstrate the safety of their product or technology before regulatory approval is granted.

4 Allow full public access to the information upon which federal regulators base approval of a product or technology.

5 Strictly enforce the ban on direct-to-consumer advertising of prescription drugs.

6 Terminate all partnerships and promotional activities so regulatory agencies regulate only in the public interest and not in the interests of the regulated.

Prime Minister, we are appealing to you for moral leadership into the 21st century so that powerful economic interests cannot trump the protection of citizens' health in Canada and throughout the world. As the Royal Society of Canada's Expert Panel on GM food reminded us, it is better to err on the side of protecting human and environmental safety than to err on the side of the risks.

Sincerely,

Shirley Douglas, O.C., Actor, Spokesperson, Canadian Health Coalition

Margaret Atwood, C.C., LLD, Author, Toronto

Ursula Franklin, O.C., PhD, Professor Emeritus, University of Toronto

Jane Jacobs, O.C., Author, Concerned Citizen, Toronto

David Suzuki, O.C., PhD, Director, David Suzuki Foundation, Vancouver

Patricia Baird, O.C., MD, Professor of Medicine, University of British Columbia

Victor Catano, PhD, President, Canadian Association of University Teachers, Ottawa

Robert Evans, PhD, Professor of Economics, University of British Columbia

Ken Georgetti, President, Canadian Labour Congress, Ottawa

Graeme Gibson, C.M., Author, Toronto

David Healy, MD, Reader in Psychological Medicine, University College of Medicine, Wales

Michele Landsberg, Writer, Journalist, Toronto

Joel Lexchin, MD, York University, Toronto

E.A. McCulloch, O.C., MD, FRS, Toronto

Barbara Mintzes, PhD, University of British Columbia

David Nathan, MD, Professor of Medicine, Harvard Medical School, Boston, U.S.A.

Nancy Olivieri, MD, University Health Network, Toronto

Linda Silas, RN, President, Canadian Federation of Nurses Unions, Ottawa

Margaret W. Thompson, O.C., Professor Emeritus, University of Toronto

Fr. Bénédict Vanier, OSCO, Abbaye Cistercienne d'Oka, Qc

Maude Barlow, The Council of Canadians

Sir David Weatherall, FRS, Regius Prof. of Medicine Emeritus, Oxford University, U.K.

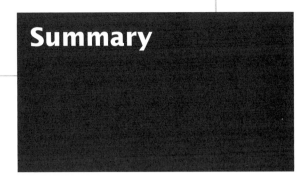

Summary

Health Canada's *Health and Safety First! A Proposal to Renew Federal Health Protection* will provide a legal framework to promote risk and lower safety standards. It will weaken or eliminate the statutory duty to protect health and safety. **If this proposal is adopted, Canadians may lose their legal right to health protection as well as recourse to the courts for Health Canada's regulatory negligence.**

Health Canada says the *Food & Drugs Act* must be "modernized" because it has a narrow focus on safety. The proposed new legislation will replace the safety focus with a focus on risk benefits. The "health" regulatory agency will promote genetically modified and "novel" food, gene therapies, bio-pharmaceuticals, reproductive technology, transplants of animal organs to humans, cloning, and life patenting. *No evidence of safety will be required.*

The unstated goal of the proposal is to bring health protection legislation in line with the government of Canada's economic policy. In effect, economic values have been given primacy over health and environmental safety. A new "Canada Health Protection Act" would:

1 shift from health protection ("duty of care") to risk management;

2 prevent the application of the Precautionary Principle where it is needed most;

3 shift the burden of proof (products are presumed safe: harm has to be proven);

4 "manage" the damage (irreversible harm and uncontrollable hazards);

5 avoid liability for regulatory negligence; and

6 allow direct-to-consumer drug advertising.

The government and industry élites have made their choice: economic growth and corporate profits are to trump the protection of citizens' health. The evidence indicates that the federal health and safety regulatory agencies have been captured by industry. These agencies and are now rigged to deceive the public. It's time for the people of Canada to take back these agencies. Canadians don't want their health protection weakened and they don't want to be lied to.

Canada's premise seems to be that "it is better that 10 hazardous products be approved to the detriment of human and environmental health than that one safe product be erroneously restricted." This helps explain why Canadian health and safety regulatory programs are open and transparent to industry, but closed and secret to the public. The Royal Society of Canada's Expert Panel on GM food warned that it is better to err on the side of human and environmental safety than to err on the side of the risk.

The future of health protection is too important to be left in the hands of "experts." **Science cannot provide definitive answers about what is dangerous or what risks society should take.** Strong public involvement in the "politics of risk" is needed to save lives, protect public health, the health of future generations, the sustainability of Medicare, and indeed the health of democracy in Canada. We shouldn't leave it to crafty corporate lobbyists in Ottawa to determine what risks are "acceptable." If we continue to let industry set our safety standards, there will literally be no limit to what they will put into our blood stream or have us swallow.

Civics writer Jane Jacobs has wise advice that can serve us well in the fight to defend our safety rights: *"Fight what is wrong. Get as many people as possible to understand. Have as good a time doing the fighting as you can."*

Recommendations

No justification exists to replace the *Food & Drugs Act* on public health grounds. A new "Health Protection Act" will result in weaker health protection in Canada. Instead of gutting the current law, there is an urgent need for better enforcement; for regulation of biotechnology and genetically modified food based on the Precautionary Principle; and for adequate public resources and scientific capacity for health protection. The following is a list of key recommendations for change:

1   Give the Minister of Health a mandate from the Prime Minister to: a) enforce the *Food & Drugs Act*, b) uphold the statutory "duty of care," and c) terminate Health Protection Legislative Renewal.

2   Adopt the Precautionary Principle as the basis of a broad, transparent, and independent assessment of risk in order to protect those least able to defend themselves from the health hazards of pharmaceuticals, genetic engineering, reproductive technologies, chemicals, and pesticides.

3   Restore the burden of proof on industry to demonstrate the safety of their product or technology and remove the burden on the public to prove harm.

4 Adhere to prescriptive, command and control regulation with mandatory compliance; and rebuild independent surveillance, testing, inspection, and enforcement programs that are necessary to fulfill Health Canada's statutory "duty of care."

5 Establish in-house scientific expertise and laboratory capacities for independent food, drug, and biotechnology research; and terminate the regulator's reliance on the industries it regulates for "scientific" information and risk assessment "strategies" – as recommended by Justice Horace Krever.

6 Terminate all partnerships and promotional activities and collusion between federal regulatory agencies and the industries they regulate (e.g., secret meetings).

7 Allow full public access to the information upon which federal regulators base approval of a product or technology, including laboratory, animal, and clinical studies, as well as the reviewers' assessments of these studies and their rationale for decisions.

8 Place an immediate moratorium on all genetically modified food and develop the scientific capacity to start testing these products for safety.

9 Place an immediate ban on the non-therapeutic use of antibiotics, hormones, and other toxic chemicals in agriculture.

10 Enforce the International Code of Marketing of Breast-Milk Substitutes and terminate all Health Canada joint event sponsorships with manufacturers of infant formula.

11 Maintain and enforce the ban on direct-to-consumer advertising of prescription drugs.

12 Establish an independent Drug Safety Board to monitor the safety of users of pharmaceuticals and to investigate the thousands of deaths each year from adverse drug reactions.

Introduction and Background

RISK FIRST, SAFETY LAST!

Health Canada is conducting a national consultation and comprehensive review of its health protection legislation "with a view to replacing outdated statutes with a new health protection legislative regime, better suited to modern technology and society." Health Canada's proposal – *Health and Safety First!* – is written in doublespeak – language intended to deceive, to mislead, and to confuse, using not simply words but orchestrated strategies of contradiction. The proposed "General Safety Requirement," for example, does not require any evidence of safety.

The reason the *Food & Drugs Act* is considered "outdated" and not "suited to modern technology" is, in the words of Health Canada internal documents, because it has "too narrow a focus on safety." The current Act "does not allow for taking into account of considerations other than safety and efficacy in managing health risks." The *Food & Drugs Act* puts safety first. *Health Canada's proposal puts safety last and profits first.*

In late 1994, the government published *Building a More Innovative Economy*, a strategy to promote job creation and economic growth. The strategy identified biotechnology and food, health and therapeutic products as the top economic sectors for "improving the efficiency of regulation." The goal is to "unleash business energies" and to "reduce the regulatory burden on business" to create jobs and growth. The biotechnology, food and drug industries themselves identified the kinds of changes to health protection legislation and regulation they wanted the federal government to make. (*http://www.ic.gc.ca*).

SMART REGULATION OR SAFE REGULATION?

According to Health Canada's 2003-2004 Report on Plans and Priorities, "the Department is responding to the 2002 Speech from the Throne's commitment to smart regulation by examining the Food & Drugs Act, its regulations, and portions of other legislation such as the Canadian Environmental Protection Act." (*http://www.tbs-sct.gc.ca/est-pre/20032004/hlth-sant/hlthsantr34_e.asp#29*). The 2002 Speech from the Throne announced a "Smart Regulation Strategy" because "the knowledge economy requires new approaches to how we regulate." The new approach is to "smart" (as opposed to "safe") regulation. The purpose of regulation will be to "contribute to innovation and economic growth, and reduce the administrative burden on business" (*http://www. sft-ddt.gc.ca/sft.htm*). In addition, "this strategy...will speed up the regulatory process for drug approvals" in order to boost pharmaceutical sales and profits.

"Smart" regulation is market-friendly regulation designed to bring regulatory regimes in line with trade and investment policy (*www.smartregulation.gc.ca*). Instead of government regulation intervening in the market, the market will now intervene in government regulation. Justice Horace Krever – who led the inquiry into the tainted blood disaster that killed thousands of Canadians – recommended *safe* regulation, not "market-oriented, trade and investment-friendly regulation." Putting profits before safety is what caused the horrendous blood disaster in Canada.

AVOIDING LIABILITY

The proposed changes to the health protection legislation are claimed to be necessary in order to pursue economic policy objectives while avoiding legal liability for regulatory negligence. Since

1990, federal courts have held that regulatory authorities have a "duty of care" and that a high standard of care is necessary to fulfill this duty. The constitutional basis of the *Food & Drugs Act* is the federal government's criminal law power.

Health Canada is currently exposed to claims for regulatory negligence in the range of $12 billion for tainted blood and faulty medical devices. Chief Justice Antonio Lamer, in swearing in new Justice Louise Arbour in 1999, predicted that biotechnology – cloning, reproductive technology, and genetic engineering – will be the legal frontier of the 21st century.

In order to abandon the high standard of care required in the *Food & Drugs Act* and replace it with "Smart Regulation" and lower standards while avoiding greater liability, legislative "renewal" is needed. This means dropping the "duty of care" in the *Food & Drugs Act*. Health Canada will not show its hand on this matter until draft legislation is tabled in the House of Commons. If Canadians lose the *Food & Drugs Act*, they could lose recourse to the courts for claims for regulatory negligence.

SHIFT THE BURDEN OF PROOF

Health Canada's proposal will replace the current health and safety standard of the *Food & Drugs Act* – requiring proof of safety – with a weaker industry standard requiring proof of harm. The presumption is that technology and products are safe unless proven otherwise. The policy of shifting the burden of proof has no legal basis until the *Food & Drug Act* is replaced. The proposal to adopt a "General Safety Requirement" in a new Act is designed to shift the burden of proof off industry onto the public. In Orwellian fashion, the General Safety Requirement (GSR) does not require evidence of safety. Instead, the public is required to demonstrate evidence of harm.

The GSR proposal says: "The Act would prohibit the manufacture, promotion, or marketing of any product which can reasonably be foreseen to cause injury..." (p.26). It defines "reasonably foreseeable conditions" as conditions "that can reasonably be expected to occur" (p.19). Under a GSR, the safety standard translates as "safe enough to be acceptable," leaving plenty of room to avoid liability. Health Canada is "selling" the entire proposal as "improved health protection" and safety standards based on the General Safety Requirement. How, one might ask, does the public get a higher level of protection from a lower standard of safety?

PREVENT PRECAUTION

The *Food & Drugs Act* is seen to be not "suited to modern technology" because it requires demonstration of safety before a product or technology can be approved. Implicit in this provision of the *Food & Drugs Act* is the Precautionary Principle. The Precautionary Principle says that the primary burden of proof is on those who would introduce new technologies, like genetically modified (GM) food, to carry out the full range of safety tests to demonstrate that they do not pose unacceptable risks to humans, animals, and the environment. In the face of scientific uncertainty, the Precautionary Principle gives explicit priority to human and environmental health.

The Precautionary Principle, and indeed most current health protection legislation, are incompatible with the economic policy objective of commercializing biotechnology products without first establishing their safety. The European Union has banned the importation of untested, unlabelled, uninsured Canadian GM food products. GM food has been approved in Canada and has been mixed into the food supply, including baby food and infant formula, without a rigorous assessment of safety. The Expert Panel on Food Biotechnology of the Royal Society of Canada established the fact that Health Canada and the Canadian Food Inspection Agency (CFIA) exempted GM food products currently on the market from rigorous scientific assessment. The Panel concluded that this approach to the regulation of food biotechnology is "scientifically unjustifiable and inconsistent with precautionary regulation of the technology."

The enforcement of the *Food & Drugs Act* and the application of the Precautionary Principle would result in a rigorous, science-based and transparent approval process. This is required because the technology involves unknown risk and the possibility of uncontrollable hazards and irreversible harm. Approval of GM food

Managing Risk?

Risk, in the technical use of the word, applies only when both probabilities and outcomes can be well defined. Since, by definition, we typically have little knowledge about the impact of new technologies, it is impossible fully to quantify any associated risks: we are dealing with uncertainty. Moreover, where we do not even know the range and character of potential impacts and the different combinations in which these might occur, we are dealing with both uncertainty and ignorance.

–Economic & Social Research Council, "The Politics of GM Food", Sussex, U.K, 1999 (*www.gecko.ac.uk*)

based on evidence of safety, as the current law requires, would take many years because there is currently no science available to verify the safety of the technology or any of its products.

PROFITS BEFORE SAFETY

Another key reason the federal government wants to dismantle the *Food & Drugs Act* is to introduce direct-to-consumer prescription drug advertising in Canada, and to expand advertising of foods, natural health food products, over-the-counter medicines and medical devices to include claims that they can prevent, treat or cure serious diseases. These two activities are currently forbidden in the Act as a health protection measure that limits manufacturers' ability to advertise products that cannot be sold freely to the public because of inherent risks (in the case of prescription drugs), and that limits manufacturers' ability to take advantage of the vulnerability of seriously ill people, for example by using fear of death and future disability to sell a product. Canadians want unbiased comparative information about medical treatments, not advertising. These changes are being recommended for one reason only: *to boost profits*.

Precautionary Principle

"In essence, the principle advises that, in the face of scientific uncertainty or lack of knowledge, it is better to err on the side of protecting human and environmental safety than to err on the side of the risks (i.e. 'Better safe than sorry.').

"The Precautionary Principle is a rule about handling uncertainty in the assessment and management of risk, and the rule recommends that the uncertainty be handled in favour of certain values – health and environmental safety – over others. Uncertainty in science produces the possibility of error in the prediction of risks and benefits. The Precautionary Principle makes the assumption that, if our best predictions turn out to be in error, it is better to err on the side of safety. That is to say, all other things being equal, it is better to have forgone important benefits of a technology by wrongly predicting risks of harm to health or the environment than to have experienced those serious harms by wrongly failing to predict them." –*Royal Society of Canada Expert Panel of Food Biotechnology, 2001*

The Krever Inquiry into the tainted blood disaster that killed thousands of Canadians illustrated the Precautionary Principle

MANAGE THE DAMAGE

The current proposal has the same objectives as Health Canada's 1998 proposal "Shared Responsibilities, Shared Vision: Renewing the Federal Health Protection Legislation." The strategic objective of Health Canada that the current proposal is designed to meet is "Managing Risks to Health" instead of the strategic objective of protecting health. Current and previous proposals are designed as a smokescreen to deceive the public. The real goal – putting economic goals ahead of health and safety – is indefensible. The declared goal – "putting health and safety first" – is doublespeak. Nowhere in the document are specific changes proposed that would lead to greater public safety.

by saying: "An action to reduce risk should not await scientific certainty." Canada actively resists the application of the Precautionary Principle in regulating genetically modified food, reproductive technology, pharmaceuticals, asbestos, pesticides, and growth hormones in meat. Canada ignored the tragic lessons of the tainted blood scandal and still places economic values over health and environmental safety.

In 2003, Canada took legal action in a WTO court in an effort to force Europeans to eat GM food against their will. Trade Minister Pettigrew said the EU's use of the Precautionary Principle (to impose a moratorium on GM food) is "not based on a scientific risk assessment." Canada's case was preposterous in light of the fact that its own regulatory approval of GM food is "scientifically unjustifiable," according to the Royal Society of Canada. Furthermore, the *Canadian Environmental Protection Act* states that, *under the laws of Canada, the government must apply the precautionary principle...Where there are threats of serious or irreversible damage,* lack of full scientific certainty shall not be used as reason for postponing cost-effective measures to prevent environmental degradation." –*Auditor-General of Canada, Dec. 2000 Ch 24, par.54. (www.oag-bvg.gc.ca)*

The proposed legislative changes are the latest stage in de-regulating and privatizing Canada's health protection system. Earlier stages include the shift to voluntary compliance, industry self-regulation, and paper audits instead of rigorous inspection. In recent years some of the physical structures have been dismantled, including the break-up of the former Health Protection Branch into three pieces, the elimination of the name "Protection" from the new branch, the weakening of scientific lab capacity and budgets for product safety research, and the transfer of health inspectors to an agency whose primary function is food promotion.

Federal food and drug safety agencies (Health Canada and the CFIA) are now running little more than "optics" programs: industry promotion and corporate public relations campaigns instead of protecting the health of Canadians. Health protection requires objective knowledge that is derived from transparent processes and is open to criticism from all informed quarters. Canada, however, has cut itself off from that kind of scientific process. The individual regulators who act on the basis of "old-fashioned" values like upholding the law and protecting public safety are gagged, harassed, disciplined, and removed from their duties.(*http://reports.fja.gc.ca/fc/2001/pub/v2/2001fc27277.html*) The new policy objective is designed to give the public a false sense of confidence in the safety of food, drugs, and medical devices: "not what is, but what appears to be." Federal regulatory agencies have been captured by the industries they are supposed to regulate. This is all part of the "Getting Government Right" ideology, in this case, getting government right out of the health protection field and into the business promotion business.

TRANSPARENCY OR SECRECY?

Health Canada is in a conflict of interest because it promotes the industries it regulates. This seriously compromises the integrity of its regulatory decision-making as well as the public's trust. The more the Minister of Health limits free access to the data upon which departmental decisions are based, the more compromised becomes the claim that the regulatory process is "science-based" or trustworthy. If data is secret, it is not science. Once the government has adopted a policy goal of economic growth through bio-technical "advances," it ceases to pursue the knowledge needed to protect people's health. In any event, science has serious limits. For instance, scientists do not yet have the framework needed to discover the long-term risks of GM foods. In such circumstances, the Precautionary Principle, which puts the burden of proof on technical innovations, is the only responsible course of action.

The legislative "renewal" document promises more transparent regulatory procedures. But does this mean greater transparency for the public, or just for industry? Real transparencyis needed but it does not require legislative change. Policy judgment and a broad definition of "commercial confidentiality" limit public access to the information on which regulatory decisions are made. It's hard to see how getting rid of the *Food & Drugs Act* would strengthen transparency or health protection. Besides, with industry dominating the machinery of government in Ottawa, it is not the time to open up health protection legislation.

THE POLITICS OF RISK

The Auditor-General has talked about the politics of risk this way: "The extent of resources allocated to reducing a specific risk is often heavily influenced by the public's tolerance of loss of life or injury." Since an injury to one is an injury to all, let's not wait until Health Canada's regulatory negligence contributes to the death of a loved one before taking action. The Canadian Health Coalition encourages citizens to critically examine Health Canada's proposal to re-write health protection legislation. The Minister of Health has said he wants to hear from Canadians on such questions as "how health authorities should respond to scientific uncertainty regarding risks to human health." Before drafting new legislation, the current public consultation will provide the government an opportunity to assess how much health protection authority it can abdicate and at what political cost.

Risks and benefits are often unknown and unevenly distributed. Who determines what risk is acceptable? How will risk be distributed in society? Who benefits from all the risk and deception in industrial food production? Who benefits from a culture of secrecy that risks lives? This is what the politics of risk is all about. In the words of the previous Deputy Minister of Health, David Dodge, it is "a very nasty business." (*www.healthcoalition. ca/nasty.html*).

The politics of risk is dominated by industry (chemical, pharmaceutical, nuclear, biotechnology, and food) and the politicians they finance. For information on politicians' secret bank accounts, see Democracy Watch's Money in Politics Campaign: (*www.dwatch.ca/camp/moneydir.html*). This Guide is intended to serve as a public education tool to help de-code Health Canada's Proposal to Renew Federal Health Protection Legislation (*http:// renewal.hc-sc.gc.ca*).

Risk = Health Hazards + $$$$

The language of risk assessment and cost-benefit analysis became central features of environmental and health regulation in the U.S. under the Reagan administration in the early 1980s. Cost-benefit analysis and risk assessment were introduced by the Mulroney government into Health Canada's Health Protection Branch. These features were formalized by the Chrétien government in the mid-1990s. They operate like a "corporate" virus that attacks the regulatory system and turns guardians of health into promoters of risk. Health Canada has no legal authority for this dangerous policy shift. This might explain why it created a *Health Products and Food Litigation Secretariat* in 2000.

When Health Canada uses the word risk, it means the "benefits" of *health hazards*. Why this focus on assessing, managing, and communicating health hazards? Health Canada has a statutory "duty of care," so why is it not focusing on: protection from, prevention of, and alternatives to health hazards? To find the answer, *follow the money*. Health Canada's "clients" are now the multi-billion-dollar pharmaceutical, food, chemical, pesticide, biotechnology, and medical device industries.

In the narrow world of cost-benefit analysis, health hazard "benefits" have paramountcy over the "cost" of ill-health, sickness, and deaths. The money's in "risk and disease management," not health promotion and disease prevention. *From 1994 to 1996, 1,450,000,000 pounds of toxic chemicals were released into the environment in Canada.* The "benefits" (money and jobs) are in selling hazardous substances. This economic activity makes people sick and creates a market for selling products to "manage" the diseases caused by the hazardous substances. The business world calls this "synergy." Health economists call it a "perverse economic incentive."

Each year, GlaxoSmithKline sells drugs worth £3,191,000,000 aimed at the cancer and respiratory market. In 2001, the Glaxo (UK) chair was also a director of a mining and minerals giant accused of causing cancers and respiratory diseases. Other directors on Glaxo's UK board included a director of Imperial Tobacco and a director of food giant Sara Lee. Glaxo was asked if the industrial interests of its directors (tobacco, alcohol, polluting firms, and companies that promote high sugar and fat diets which contribute to diabetes and heart disease) showed they were more interested in making money than making people healthy. The firm's spokesperson replied that "directors do have responsibilities to their shareholders" (*The Ecologist*, October 2001).

Before the rise of the language of risk assessment in the 1970s, health concerns were talked about in such terms as "environmental crisis," "dangerous side-effects," "health hazards," "cancer-causing chemicals," "cell damage from radioactive particles," and "exposure rates." These and similar terms have now been redefined as questions of "risk." The difference is important. *Risk is the opposite of prevention, protection, and precaution.*

If Health Canada upheld its statutory duty of care, it would speak the language of health protection and disease prevention ("stop breast cancer before it starts"). *Guiding Principles for Risk Decision-Making* is not the language of health. It is the language of corporations that profit from health hazards ("sell breast-cancer treatments"). When governments and corporations want to talk about bad things in our food, air, and water, they speak the language of risk assessment and tell us to trust the "scientific" experts who have financial ties to the companies that produce the hazards.

CHAPTER 1

Why Get Rid of The *Food And Drugs Act?*

WHAT HEALTH CANADA *SAYS*

"Health Canada can act to provide protection only within the powers entrusted to it by legislation, and that legislation needs to be updated, modernized and strengthened to keep pace with sweeping changes in society – changes that include new and emerging health risks, environmental changes, new scientific and technological discoveries, and changing expectations and attitudes." (**Health and Safety First!**, p.4)

REALITY CHECK

▶ If current health protection legislation does not provide Health Canada with health protection powers, why have the courts in Canada held that Health Canada and other regulatory authorities have a "duty of care" and that a high standard of care is necessary to fulfill this duty? Courts have also ruled that the powers entrusted to Health Canada in legislation (primarily the *Food & Drugs Act*) and the "duty of care" cannot be abdicated through a change in policy (shifting to risk and abandoning health protection). This is why Health Canada is trying to change health protection legislation so that it can "legally" abandon its duty of care.

Why New Legislation – Myth vs. Fact

Myth: *"Legislation needs to be modernized...to keep pace with sweeping changes."*

Fact: This is not a goal. Safety and the "duty of care" do not go out of date and should not be compromised for economic ends.

Myth: *"Health protection will be strengthened in the new legislation."*

Fact: The changes proposed will *weaken* health protection.

Myth: *"Legislation needs to be streamlined."*

Fact: There will still be several health protection laws.

Myth: *"Enforcement and compliance mechanisms are inadequate."*

Fact: The problem of Health Canada not enforcing a good law will not be solved by introducing a bad law.

Myth: New legislation will *"render Health Canada's review processes more transparent."*

Fact: Excessive secrecy at Health Canada is policy, not law.

▶ Why is it assumed that current legislation must automatically adapt to "sweeping changes" and "technological discoveries"? This unwarranted assumption is code for the government's biotechnology strategy. "Biotechnology," Canadians are told, "will figure prominently in Canada's future" and so "Canada must position itself to be a leader." With this economic priority established, a regulatory regime to serve the business agenda will be fashioned. Justice Krever warned that health regulatory authorities must regulate only in the interest of the public. Health Canada has stood the Krever Report on its head and is regulating in the interests of the regulated (i.e., the Canadian biotechnology industry). There is no public policy discussion of who will benefit and who will reap the harm of unregulated biotechnology. Instead,

Food & Drugs Act: "too focused on safety"

This is what Health Canada is claiming: "The Act is outdated and needs to be reviewed. For one thing, it is not well enough adapted to deal with a number of issues raised by modern technology such as the use of human organs for medical purposes, genetically engineered products, xenotransplants, etc.

"The Act does not allow for the taking into account of considerations other than safety and efficacy in managing health risk (ethical issues; social, economic and cultural considerations; need to improve the economy and to promote competitiveness, etc.)..."

Source: Health Canada, "Food And Drugs Act," document obtained through Access to Information by Ken Rubin for the Canadian Health Coalition, April 24, 1998. (*http://www.healthcoalition.ca/overhaul-FDA. html*).

"The Canada We Want" is technologically predetermined. Where is the democratic debate, the examination of alternatives, the ethical analysis, or an honest cost-benefit analysis?

▶ Implicit in the *Food & Drugs Act* is the Precautionary Principle. Under this *Act*, the proponents of products and technology must first demonstrate evidence of safety before approval. This focus on safety in the *Food & Drugs Act* is precisely what the Royal Society of Canada's Expert Panel on Food Biotechnology (RSC) said was required now more than ever. It is also precisely what Health Canada wants to remove under the guise of "modernizing" the legislation. The 2001 RSC Report concluded: "The recommendations contained in this Report assume that the fundamental tenets of the Precautionary Principle should be respected in the management of the risks associated with food biotechnology.

Food & Drugs Act: "ill-suited to trade"

"The extent to which Canada's legislative framework is fostering a pro-competitive regulatory environment is somewhat unclear, and certain aspects may be hindering Canada's pursuit of greater market openness. Although the WTO and other trade agreements have served as important drivers of regulatory reform on this issue, current design features of Canadian legislation may be inhibiting their implementation in practice. For example, many current legislative frameworks do not include authority for the development of performance-based regulation – an important tool for avoiding unnecessary trade restrictiveness. Regulators are thus faced with the obligation to use performance-based requirements as the basis of domestic regulation wherever possible, but lack the legal authority to do this in practice. As a result, *major pieces of legislation, such as the Food and Drugs Act, often constrain regulators to adhere to the command-and-control, prescriptive style of regulation and perpetuate an old-style approach ill-suited to the dynamics of good regulatory practice in general and trade and investment-friendliness in particular.* And even where there have been moves to build more flexibility into regulatory compliance (an approach once embraced but ultimately defeated in the proposal for a *Regulatory Efficiency Act*), the power of special interest groups to dissuade government from trusting business to "do the right thing" to achieve a regulatory objective risks paralyzing government's intentions in this area."

(In other words, democracy and the common good keep getting in the way of corporate rule and greed. Common sense says you don't put the fox in charge of the henhouse.)

Source: OECD, "Enhancing Market Openness Through Regulatory Reform," Review of Regulatory Reform in Canada, 2002, p. 59 (*http://www.oecd.org/dataoecd/48/26/1960546.pdf*) Emphasis added.

All of these recommendations can be implemented within the existing regulatory framework." (*http://www.rsc.ca/foodbiotechnology/indexEN.html*).

Health Canada's reasons for replacing the *Food & Drugs Act* do not hold up after close examination of the details in the proposal.

WHAT IT *REALLY* MEANS

What are the *real reasons* for Health Canada's proposed legislative changes? The evidence suggests that the changes will provide the legal basis and authority for "Smart" Regulation ("market-oriented, trade- and investment-friendly"). The new legislation will:

- shift from health protection ("duty of care") to risk management;
- prevent the application of the Precautionary Principle;
- shift the burden of proof ("General Safety Requirement:);
- "manage" the damage (irreversible harm and uncontrollable hazards);
- avoid liability for regulatory negligence; and
- allow direct-to-consumer drug advertising.

CHAPTER 2

"Smart" Regulation or Safe Regulation?

"SMART" REGULATION

The 2002 Speech from the Throne announced a smart regulation strategy "that would promote health and sustainability, contribute to innovation and economic growth, and reduce the administrative burden on business." The 2003 Federal Budget provided $4 million over two years to fund an External Advisory Committee "to recommend areas where government needs to redesign its regulatory approach to create and maintain a Canadian advantage." The Prime Minister appointed a former senior executive with leading food processing companies as the new chair of the Advisory Committee. *www.smartregulation.gc.ca*

According to the OECD, "smart regulation" means "market-oriented, trade- and investment-friendly regulation: "OECD Member countries now have at their disposal a growing body of knowledge on trade-relevant best practices for enhancing market openness through regulatory reform; the next phase of regulatory reform "should be 'smart' regulation...designed to ensure mutual coherence and complementarity between regulatory and trade policy regimes." – Working Party of the Trade Committee, "Integrating market Openness into the Regulatory Process", 17 February, 2003 (*http://www.olis.oecd.org/*).

Smart regulation is the next phase of deregulation. But in Canada it is officially (and euphemistically) called "the next phase in regulatory reform." Smart regulation in health and safety regulatory agencies will require "changes in regulatory culture." A good example of the new culture at Health Canada is the biotechnology entrepreneur recently appointed to head the Office of Chief Scientist. Guardians and traders have very different cultures. Traders should not be put in charge of the safety of the blood, water, food and air supply, unless you are willing to accept avoidable deaths.

Canadians are not prepared to support federal privatization, harmonization, and deregulation in the area of human and environmental health and safety. This is especially true after the tainted blood disaster, incidents of drinking water contamination across Canada, and the food safety threats from Mad Cow and E-coli. The government knows this and so, to reassure us, they lie and claim that smart regulation will "promote health." We are not told how. This is the sugar-coating on the poison pill. The grim truth is that smart regulation – which most Canadians would consider anything but smart – puts profits before health.

When you try to mix the federal trade regime in with the health and safety regulatory regime – the real objective of "smart" regulation – you create what Jane Jacobs calls a "monstrous hybrid." These two regimes do contradictory types of work and are prone to corruption if they stray across either their functional or moral barriers. **The purpose of health protection legislation is to safeguard health and safety, *not* trade and investment interests.** When the Government of Canada mixes trade policy into health protection functions, lives are unconscionably put at risk.

QUESTIONS

2.1 Why does Health Canada's proposal for legislative "renewal" ignore or misrepresent: a) the 1997 Krever Report into Tainted Blood; b) the 1998 public consultation on health protection renewal; c) the Minister's Science Advisory Board reports; d) the Auditor-General of Canada's Reports; and e) the recommenda-

"$mart Regulation" vs. Safe Regulation

"$mart Regulation"	Safe Regulation
• Trader ethic	• Guardian ethic
• Exploiting vulnerability	• Protecting the vulnerable
• Business culture	• Safety culture
• Burden of proof of harm	• Burden of responsibility
• Business standards (GSR)	• "Duty of care" standards
• Self-regulation	• Command and control
• Self-reporting & "audits"	• Independent inspections and
• Voluntary compliance	testing
• Voluntary labelling	• Mandatory compliance
• Free-market (prison blood, BSE in feed, untested GM food)	• Mandatory labelling
	• Ban trade in poisonous products (especially biohazards)
• Manage the damage (downstream)	• First, do no harm (upstream)
• Protect products	• Protect people
• Sell breast cancer treatments	• Stop breast cancer before it starts

tions of the Royal Society of Canada Expert Panel on Food Biotechnology?

2.2 Why is the Minister of Health promoting a trade and industry agenda ("Smart" regulation), when his statutory duty is to protect Canadians' health? If the Minister of Health won't protect health, who in the Government of Canada will?

2.3 How many lives are government and business élites prepared to sacrifice on the altars of *innovation*, *competitiveness*, the *knowledge-based economy*, and *biotechnology*?

2.4 Does "integrating market openness into the regulatory process" at Health Canada mean that trade in HIV blood from an Arkansas jail and BSE-infected animal feed from the U.K. will henceforth be considered examples of "smart" regulation?

CHAPTER 3

Krever and the Auditor-General on Legislative Change

WHAT HEALTH CANADA *SAYS*

"*Every independent review of the health protection system since 1992, including the Krever Inquiry into tainted blood, has recommended changes to the legislation under which Health Canada operates.*" (**Health and Safety First!**, p. 4).

The references to the Krever Report and the 1999, 2000 and 2002 Reports of the Auditor-General imply that these authorities endorse Health Canada's proposal to re-write the health protection legislation. *Nothing could be further from the truth.*

REALITY CHECK

▸ The Krever Report, 1997, made no recommendations to change legislation. Instead, Justice Krever recommended changes to the *Food and Drug Regulations*. Justice Krever blamed the blood disaster on massive abdication of regulatory authority, not on faulty legislation (*http://www.hc-sc.gc.ca/english/protection/krever/*).

▸ The restructuring of Health Canada's health protection system, as well as current proposals, betray the spirit and the letter of the Krever Inquiry. Justice Krever said a major cause of the blood disaster – which killed thousands of Canadians – was *the reliance of Health Canada regulators on outside information.* Health Canada did not decide independently whether to use its authority to require that measures be taken to reduce risk. In effect, Health Canada "made itself dependent on an organization whose activities it was supposed to regulate." "*The relationship between the regulator and the regulated…must never become one in which the regulator loses sight of the principle that it regulates only in the public interest and not in the interest of the regulated.*" – Krever Report, Vol. 3, p. 995, emphasis added. In ignoring Krever's warning that regulators get back to the mission of health protection, not industrial promotion, Health Canada is trying to turn vice into virtue.

Why has Health Canada failed so miserably to meet the standard of care described by the Auditor-General?

▶ Since 1990, the courts have held that regulatory authorities have a "duty of care" and that a high standard of care is necessary to fulfill this duty. As a result, Health Canada is more exposed to claims for regulatory negligence. There are currently several billions of dollars in negligence claims against Health Canada for tainted blood, unsafe drugs, and faulty medical devices. The Auditor-General of Canada (AG) issued a warning in 2000 that "the government is exposing itself to very high risks" because of deregulation, industry self-regulation policies, and the failure to monitor against objectives.

▶ "To reduce the risk of regulatory negligence, regulatory authorities need to take a variety of measures to provide an appropriate standard of care. For example, they must ensure the following in given circumstances: human resources are sufficient;

decisions to delegate are well-founded; risk management strategies are defensible; compliance and enforcement policies standards are practical; regulation delegated to industry is properly monitored against objectives; testing and approval procedures reflect recent technological standards; timely action is taken to prevent public harm; and timely advice is given to the public on dangerous products or activities." (Auditor-General of Canada, *Federal Health and Safety Regulatory Programs*, ch. 24, par. 59, Dec. 2000, www.oag-bvg.gc.ca)

WHAT IT *REALLY* MEANS

▶ A Health Canada document obtained by the Canadian Health Coalition through Access to Information explains the real reason for wanting to change health protection legislation. According to this document, the Food and Drugs Act is not suited to deal with emerging technologies like genetically modified food because it has a "narrow focus on safety." The document states: "The Act does not allow for the taking into account of considerations other than safety and efficacy in managing health risk". (*http://www.healthcoalition.ca/overhaul-FDA.html*). This is a core objective of the "Proposal to Renew Federal Health Protection Legislation."

▶ There has never been an independent review of Health Canada's ability to protect the public under the Food and Drug Act. Neither Justice Krever nor the Auditor-General has called for legislative changes to weaken the Minister's statutory duty to protect the public's health. Instead, the food, drug, and biotechnology industries, and the politicians they fund, press for changes to Health Canada's legislation in order to "position Canada competitively within emerging international regulatory standards" by weakening provisions in the *Food and Drug Act*.

3.1 Does the Minister of Health expect Canadians to believe that the proposal to "*Renew Federal Health Protection Legislation*" is the "result of lessons learned from the Krever Inquiry"? Is the attempt to dump liability for regulatory negligence one of the lessons learned?

3.2 Why has Health Canada failed to act on the necessary measures identified by the Auditor-General of Canada to provide an appropriate standard of care in order to save lives and reduce the risk of regulatory negligence?

3.3 Where is the evidence to support the statement that Justice Krever and the Auditor-General "recommended changes to the legislation under which Health Canada operates"?

CHAPTER 4

"Changes to Strengthen and Renew"

WHAT HEALTH CANADA *SAYS*

"Over the past few years, a number of changes have been made to strengthen and renew the health protection program." (**Health and Safety First!**, p. 3)

REALITY CHECK

▶ Health Canada quietly dismantled the entire Bureau of Drug Research in 1997. Before the systematic erosion of in-house independent scientific and laboratory research, Health Canada drug scientists used to be recognized internationally for research on drug quality, toxicity, bio-equivalence, allergenicity, natural products, and clinical application of drugs.

▶ The scientific deficit in drug safety at Health Canada was followed by a cost recovery program whereby a major part of the budget for the evaluation of new drugs comes from drug company user fees. This makes the Therapeutic Products Directorate at Health Canada dependent on the industry it regulates. In 2003-2004, Health Canada received $40.7 million from the pharmaceutical industry in user fees. With this kind of cost-recovery came a new operational principle for Health Canada drug reviewers:

CLIENT = INDUSTRY. The public is now relegated to the status of just one of many "stakeholders."

▶ Also in 1997, food safety research projects were terminated and investigative labs secretly dismantled. Food safety research and surveillance staff positions have decreased from approximately 40 to 29 in recent years. Food safety research cuts included: investigations into detection of deadly microorganisms and harmful bacteria, toxic chemicals, preservatives, pesticides, residues of volatile contaminants, additives, herbicides, insecticides, and genetically modified organisms in food.

▶ In 2000, after deep cuts to scientific research and surveillance, the Health Protection Branch was broken into three separate pieces, including a new Health Products and Food Branch. The word "protection" was symbolically dropped from the Branch's name. This reflects the shift in mandate from "old-fashioned" values of health protection to the "Getting Government Right" values of risk-benefit management. In other words, risk will be managed to benefit Health Canada's new client: industry. The risk Health Canada says it is managing is preventable injury and death. This radical shift took place in spite of strong public opposition and warnings from the Krever Inquiry.

▶ Recent cuts to strategic food safety research include the "Total Diet Study," which measures the total intake of pesticides and other chemicals in the human diet in Canada. As a result, recent results for levels of pesticide dietary intake have a six-year gap in the data. Chemicals in the diet of Canadians leading to higher cancer rates are designated by Health Canada senior managers as having a low priority.

▶ The recent report of the Environment Commissioner said the Pest Management Regulatory Agency (PMRA), a branch of Health Canada, is not managing pesticides effectively, nor can it honestly say that pesticide use in Canada is safe. In 1999, the federal government said it would re-evaluate 405 active ingredients approved for use in Canadian pesticides by 2006. Since then,

Health Minister: Toxic Metals in Food Not A Health Threat

Health Minister McLellan says toxic metals in food not a health threat
By Dennis Bueckert –Canadian Press, May 5, 2003.

OTTAWA (CP) Health Minister Anne McLellan says levels of toxic metals in Canadian foods are not high enough to pose a health risk, but environmentalists say any toxic contamination in food is too much. "People shouldn't be consuming lead at any level", said Sarah Winterton of Environmental Defence Canada. "It's a highly toxic chemical, we've spent a great deal of money to get it out of gasoline, to get it out of paint and out of solder in tin cans, and we find we're still eating it in our foods."

Q. If the food and chemical industries have convinced Health Canada that eating lead is not a health risk, what else are we expected to swallow?

however, only six active ingredients have been fully re-evaluated. The PMRA acts on limited and unreliable information about actual pesticide use and impacts in the real world; its assessments are built on a foundation of assumptions. One is that users comply with label directions. This is unrealistic. The Environment Commissioner said: "The federal government has long known about many of these problems...the government's response so far leads me to question whether it takes pesticide safety concerns seriously." (*http://www.oag-bvg.gc.ca*).

▸ Health Canada is abdicating its legal duty to protect Canadians from hazardous products in food. Instead of regulating for safety, Health Canada promotes food biotechnology and has no toxicology program devoted to its safety. Health Canada does not have one single research scientist specializing in proteomics (the study of protein mutations resulting from gene insertions). The potential harm from new technology such as zenotransplantation, GM food, and gene therapies is irreversible.

▸ The former Deputy Minister of Health said in 1999 that Health Canada anticipates an increase of up to 500% in volume of biotechnology products coming to them for evaluation. *http://www.healthcoalition.ca/IC-2002-0093.pdf.* Six years later, Health Canada still has grossly inadequate scientific capacity in DNA technology assessment. Perhaps this is an example of *Smart Regulation*: avoid independent safety research in order to provide a competitive advantage for the Canadian biotechnology industry. Europeans seem to prefer safe regulation of biotechnology and have adopted the Precautionary Principle because of uncontrollable, unknown, and irreversible risks to future generations.

WHAT IT *REALLY* MEANS

▸ It is virtually impossible to enforce the provisions of the *Food and Drugs Act* without in-house investigative lab capacity and staff safety research scientists. Without credible science, health and safety regulatory programs are not trustworthy and are seen to be subservient to political policy and corporate interests. Private laboratories in Canada do not have the equipment, the multi-disciplinary teams, or the legal authority to undertake investigative and long-term research and surveillance of nonstandard problems and product safety. It is virtually impossible to find university researchers in the relevant field who do not have conflicts of interest by virtue of industry funding.

▸ When asked about the cuts to health protection safety research in a Senate investigation of the drug review process, the former Deputy Minister of Health, David Dodge, replied: "We do less ourselves with money commissioned publicly. We have chosen to use the tool of creating intellectual property rights to get the work done, as opposed to having government agencies do it themselves." (*http://www.parl.gc.ca*). This policy ignores the problem of the manipulation of scientific research by for-profit corporations. Food and drug companies and GM food manufacturers

Health Minister Bans Yo-Yo Balls

Health Minister Bans Yo-Yo Balls
News Release, October 3, 2003.

OTTAWA – The Honourable Anne McLellan, Minister of Health, today announced that the Government of Canada has implemented an immediate ban on the advertisement, sale and importation of yo-yo type balls and other similar products. This type of toy, also known as yo-yo balls, yo-balls and water yo-yo balls, has been prohibited under the *Hazardous Products Act* due to the unacceptable risk of strangulation to children.

http://www.hcsc.gc.ca/english/media/releases/2003/2003_78.htm

Q. Why does Health Canada apply the Precautionary Principle in regulating yo-yo's (a known and controllable risk) but refuse to use the Precautionary Principle in regulating GM food or pesticides (unknown, uncontrollable, and high risk affecting future generations)?

routinely place the needs of stockholders over considerations of public health. (Marion Nestle, *Food Politics: How the Food Industry Influences Nutrition and Health*, Berkeley, 2002).

▸ When Health Canada unveiled its plan to dismantle the Health Protection Branch in 2000, Deputy Minister Dodge said a key goal of the changes is "to work effectively with our external collaborators and partners." He added: "We have to tear down the walls" between government and industry. (*Ottawa Citizen*, April 18, 2000). When de-coded, this means that the regulated industries will tell the regulator that their products are safe and Health Canada will no longer have the scientists to conduct their own risk assessment.

▶ Prior to announcing the changes to the Health Protection Branch in 2000, Deputy Minister Dodge said the changes were long overdue because regulation was an old-fashioned way to deal with risk. "It's a difficult job," said Dodge. "It's the core, in some sense, of the Health Department. But it's the nasty core." (*Ottawa Citizen*, April 15, 2000).

QUESTIONS

4.1 If the recent changes to the Health Protection Branch, including the elimination of the word "protection" from the Branch's name, were designed to "*strengthen*" the health protection program, why did the Department's Deputy Minister refer to these changes as "the nasty core"?

4.2 When did the government get the mandate to shift from health protection to risk management?

4.3 Is the policy that puts a chemical giant like Monsanto in charge of researching and assessing the safety of its own products in total secrecy (genetically modified bovine growth hormone, potatoes and wheat) an example of "Smart Regulation"?

4.4 If health and safety come first at Health Canada, why were Department scientists under pressure to approve a genetically modified bovine growth hormone and then gagged and disciplined when they refused to approve the drug without data demonstrating the safety of the product as required by law?

4.5 If Health Canada ignored the call for the application of the Precautionary Principle from the Krever Inquiry and the Royal Society's Expert Panel Report on the Future of Food Biotechnology, is it reasonable for a citizen to assume the current consultation is being conducted in good faith?

CHAPTER 5

Risk Assessment

WHAT HEALTH CANADA'S PROPOSAL *SAYS*

"Guiding Principles for Risk Decision Making: The Act would also affirm key principles that would guide decisions about risks to health:
- *The assessment of risk shall be based solely on science and objective observation.*
- *Potential negative effects shall be weighed against potential advantage for the people of Canada.*
- *The concept of precaution will be applied..."*
(**Health and Safety First!**, p. 18)

REALITY CHECK

▶ Science is an indispensable but insufficient element for assessment and management of risk in the public interest. "Science should be on tap, not on top." (*Sterling*). *The precautionary approach is more scientifically rigorous than the narrow risk approach adopted by Health Canada and the* CFIA. For one thing, the precautionary approach to regulating risk technology acknowledges ignorance, uncertainty, and the potential for error, in risk assessment (risk assessors don't know what they don't know). The phrase "based solely on science" has become a catch-phrase for industry to dismiss the Precautionary Principle and claim it is "unscientific." What needs to be dismissed is the assumption that "scientific risk assessment" is not unavoidably and inextricably intertwined with subjective framing assumptions, values, ignorance, and trade-offs.

▸ The proposal that "the assessment of risk shall be based solely on science" is doublespeak. It serves two purposes. First, the notion masks the political and ethical nature of the exercise and conceals the economic influences and value-laden assumptions. Second, it displaces what should be the basis for the assessment of risk, namely *the Precautionary Principle, incorporating a transparent, independent and broad scientific appraisal, an examination of the full range of alternatives, and a comprehensive ethical analysis.*

▸ The Precautionary Principle was developed as an approach to use *when scientific knowledge is limited and incomplete.* It allows a society to be cautious when we don't know for sure. To make it subject "solely to science" turns it on its head, *limiting precaution to a last resort in the face of assured risk.* The "risk-cost-benefit" approach to safety is an industry-friendly standard that permits any level of risk (e.g., from asbestos, nuclear power, pesticides, antibiotics, growth hormones and chemical adulteration of food) as long as there are offsetting benefits for the purveyors of these products.

▸ The language of risk (risk assessment/management/communication), is *not* the language of public health. Risk assessment has been described as "the most powerful tool that the poisoners and destroyers of the planet ever invented" (*Rachel's Environment & Health Biweekly*, August 17, 2000). In the U.S. and Canada, it is used "as a weapon against that prime bíte noire of the political right, government regulation of health and safety." (*The Lancet*, February 11, 1995). Here's how it works: Decision-makers generally decide what they want to do, and, instead of examining all the alternatives, they hire a risk assessor to convince everyone that the damage they are about to do to us is "acceptable." What is acceptable is naturally a political judgment.

Assumptions, not "science," frame risk assessment

Scientific judgments on risk and uncertainties are underpinned and framed by unavoidably subjective assumptions about the nature, magnitude, and relative importance of these uncertainties. These "framing assumptions" can have an overwhelming effect on the results obtained in risk assessments. This partly explains why different risk assessments on the same issue can obtain widely varying results, even though each has apparently been conducted in accordance with the tenets of "sound science."

The adoption of any particular set of framing assumptions in risk assessment must therefore be justified. Such justification cannot be undertaken in terms of "science," but must be assessed in terms of factors such as:
• the legitimacy of the institution making the justification;
• the degree of democratic accountability to which the institution is subjected; and
• the ethical acceptability of the assumptions adopted.

Yet the assumptions embedded in risk assessments on such issues are rarely examined, despite the existence of straightforward techniques for doing so.

"Absence of evidence" of risks is not "evidence of absence."

–ESRC, "The Politics of GM Food", Sussex, U.K, 1999. *www. gecko.ac.uk*

▶ Risk assessment can provide industry with "scientific" cover for just about any damaging activity. Risk assessment is used, for example, to justify "acceptable levels" of pesticide residues, hormones, antibiotics, genetically modified organisms, pesticides, and other toxic chemicals in food. Risk assessment is not pure science. It is usually based on imperfect information, requiring assumptions to be made with a strong effect on results. It is a political mixture that can contain various ingredients: prejudices, biases, vested interests, fraud, guesses, estimates, limited scientific facts, and many value judgments – all hiding under the cover of "objective" science. Risk assessment and cost-benefit analysis became a central feature of environmental and health regulation under the Reagan administration. The Mulroney regime prepared the way for it in Canada, but it was first applied to health regulation in Canada by the Chrétien government in the mid-1990s.

▶ Risk assessment is a useful way to put together different information on what the level of potential risk of a specific chemical or other technology might be, from its toxicology, what is known about effects on people, then look at possible exposure levels both to the population as a whole and to vulnerable populations, and come up with some estimate of the potential degree

"All risk is not the same, and the public is not irrational."

–Science, No. 236, 1987

of harm. Because it is always based on incomplete information, this is an inherently uncertain modelling exercise. If done well and honestly, it should take explicit account of ignorance, uncertainty, and the potential for error. It is useful as a way to lay out what we know and don't know about the potential risks of environmental exposure, for example, and come up with educated guesses about what might happen, and in a way that is consistent with the Precautionary Principle. There are two possible pitfalls. One is when you already know what you want out of a risk assessment exercise and therefore feed in assumptions that will produce a specific result. This is easy to do, given all the uncertainties. The second pitfall is what comes after: decisions about risk management. These are easily influenced by economic aims and conflicts of interest.

▶ In dealing with risks to health, the proposal lists safety last, not first, in the guiding principles. To make the levels of precaution subject "solely to science" and then to an economic cost-benefit analysis would, in effect, negate the central point of the Precautionary Principle: to create a presumption in favour of safety. It recognizes that scientific knowledge about potential harmful effects of a new technology is often incomplete when it is first developed, and affirms the overriding principle that safety needs to come first.

▶ One key question is whose risk and whose benefit? The person sick with asbestos-related disease and the asbestos company executive are not one and the same. This approach to safety is also willing to "trade off" significant risks in order to limit the costs of safety or to realize certain economic benefits. This proposal to put risk first and safety last is required in light of the Government of Canada's regulatory agenda and the recent "Smart Regulation Strategy" to reduce the "regulatory burden" on industry.

▶ A risk cost-benefit analysis is anti-precautionary because of the built-in bias in favour of technological benefits. The benefits are immediate, highly predictable, quantifiable, and often overhyped. The risks are discounted because they tend to be long-term, less certain, and less quantifiable. There is also the problem of government eliminating scientific research into product safety and instead promoting the products they are supposed to regulate.

▶ Industry manipulates scientific research for its own ends: maximizing profits. Recent instances of corporate abuse of science include: suppression of unfavourable research results, distorted clinical trials, ghost-written "scientific" articles in peer-reviewed journals, retaliation against and intimidation of "uncooperative" scientists. ("Conference deplores corporate influence on academic science," July 26, 2003 *www.thelancet.com*). In Canada today, scientists are rewarded when they discover technological benefits, and – as in the case of Dr. Nancy Olivieri at

Toronto's Hospital for Sick Children – penalized if they discover, and try to publish, negative results (*http://jme.bmjjournals.com/ cgi/data/28/2/DC1/12*).

▸ The "Guiding Principles for Risk-Decision-Making" amount to putting profit ahead of human life. Health and safety become just another trade-off for "jobs and growth." As the Auditor-General of Canada pointed out, manufacturers do not necessarily adopt measures to avoid injuries and death where the cost of the

Precautionary Principle Index

Number of times the term

"Precautionary Principle" is used in Health Canada's

Health Protection Legislative Renewal proposal

and background documents: 0

measure is greater than the cost of settling civil actions for an injury or death. An example of this is the Ford Pinto's exploding gas tank. It cost Ford more to fix the flaw that to compensate the dead and injured, so they hesitated to "adopt measures to avoid injuries."

▸ The current policy of risk management based on secret, non-peer-reviewed "science" has no basis in law. The legal duty of the Minister of Health as provided in the *Food & Drugs Act* is to protect the health and safety of the public by requiring that product manufacturers demonstrate the safety of their products. Health Canada now says its policy is "to set risk tolerance levels." The damage we are dealing with is preventable illness, death, and environmental disaster.

▸ Health Canada is currently facing billions of dollars in liability law-suits for failing to perform its legal "duty to care." Avoiding massive legal liability is the real but unstated reason for the *Health Protection Legislative Renewal*. The current policy – secret regulation, no public accountability, and no public information

Factors of Acceptable and Unacceptable Risk

Factors of Acceptable Risk	Factors of Unacceptable Risk
• Risk-bearer gets benefits	• Risk-bearer gets no benefits
• Controllable hazard	• Uncontrollable hazard
• Hazard not catastrophic	• Catastrophic hazard
• Consequences not fatal	• Consequences fatal
• Voluntary (risk-taker)	• Involuntary (risk victim)
• Risk distributed equitably	• Risk distributed inequitably
• Low risk to future generations	• High risk to future generations
• Easily reduced	• Not easily reduced
• Observable	• Not observable
• Known to those exposed	• Unknown to those exposed
• Risk known to science	• Risk unknown to science
• Open and transparent science	• Secret "science" and data withheld
• Trustworthy risk manager	• Untrustworthy risk manager
• Risk part of ethical activity	• Risk part of unethical activity or fraud

Q. Why are the risks associated with GM Food, pesticides in food, hormones and antibiotics in meat, unlabelled potential hazards in baby food, BSE, and vCJD "acceptable" risks to Health Canada risk managers? Why are yo-yo balls an unacceptable risk?

on how Health Canada assessed the risk of a product – is bad enough. Codifying bad policy into law would be a lot worse. **If Canadians lose the *Food & Drugs Act*, they lose recourse to the courts for claims of regulatory negligence.**

QUESTIONS

5.1 If Health Canada's proposed legislation puts "safety first," as purported, why is the vague "concept of precaution" listed third

"Expert" and Public Perception of Risk

"Expert" Perception of Risk	Public Perception of Risk
• Narrow "cost-benefit" (quantitative) • Err on side of risk "benefits" • Probability of potential harm ("don't worry, it won't happen!") • Presumed safe until scientific certainty proves otherwise • "Trust us, we're experts!"	• Broad frame (qualitative) • Err on side of safety • Magnitude of potential harm ("if it happens, it will be a disaster") • Absence of evidence of harm is not evidence of safety • Common sense is trigger for survival

after two principles as guides that negate the use of precaution in risk decision-making, namely, "science-based risk assessment" and "cost-benefit analysis"?

5.2 What does the vague wording "concept of precaution will be applied" mean? If safety comes first, why is there no reference anywhere to the Precautionary Principle?

5.3 Why is the economic principle of cost-benefit analysis listed as a guide for safety assessment? If safety is in fact first, why would we weigh the negative effects on the voiceless against potential advantages for the economically powerful?

5.4 If safety and precaution come first, why are the guiding principles designed for "risk decision-making" and not for preventive management of risk and risk prevention strategies?

5.5 How is the "Fundamental Values" section of the proposal consistent with the regulatory policy, international trade positions, and risk management framework of the central agencies of the Government of Canada, all of which put risk benefits before safety?

A model of the relationships between concepts of risk, science and precaution

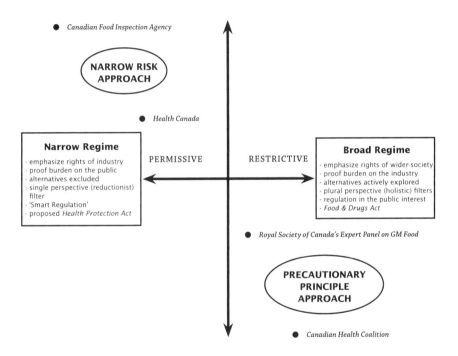

'UNSCIENTIFIC' APPRAISAL

Opaque, ad hoc, credulous, doctrinaire, partisan, secretive, unaccountable, no learning

● *Canadian Food Inspection Agency*

NARROW RISK APPROACH

● *Health Canada*

Narrow Regime
- emphasize rights of industry
- proof burden on the public
- alternatives excluded
- single perspective (reductionist) filter
- 'Smart Regulation'
- proposed *Health Protection Act*

PERMISSIVE   RESTRICTIVE

Broad Regime
- emphasize rights of wider-society
- proof burden on the industry
- alternatives actively explored
- plural perspective (holistic) filters
- regulation in the public interest
- *Food & Drugs Act*

● *Royal Society of Canada's Expert Panel on GM Food*

PRECAUTIONARY PRINCIPLE APPROACH

● *Canadian Health Coalition*

'SCIENTIFIC' APPRAISAL

Transparent, systematic, sceptical, peer-reviewed, independent, accountable, learning

CHC adaptation of Sterling, A. *On Science and Precaution in the management of technological risk*, Seville, 1999

Location of hazards derived from the relationships among 18 risk characteristics

Each factor is made up of a combination of characteristics, as indicated by the lower diagram

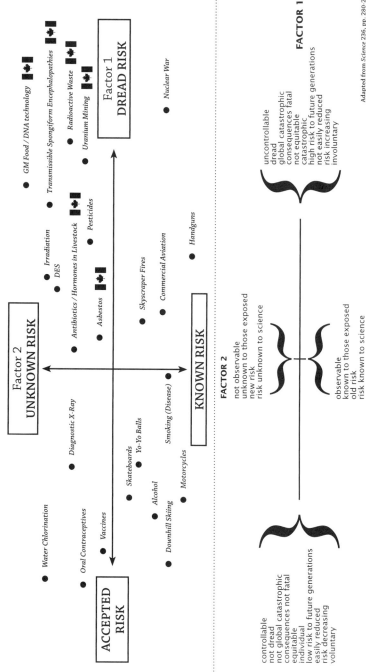

Adapted from *Science* 236, pp. 280-285

CHAPTER 6

General Safety Requirement

WHAT HEALTH CANADA'S PROPOSAL *SAYS*

"...the Act would establish a General Safety Requirement that would apply to all products...The General Safety Requirement would be articulated as follows:
- *The Act would prohibit the manufacture, promotion or marketing of any product which can reasonably be foreseen to cause injury to the health of a person for any of the reasons listed in the Act.*
- *The factors to be considered in determining whether the supplier has exercised reasonable care would include the guiding principles on risk decision-making described above"*

(**Detailed Legislative Proposal**, pp. 26-32)

The proposal (pps.19-20) defines "reasonably foreseeable conditions" as referring to conditions:
- *"• A3.8.1 – that accord with instructions or representations by the supplier...*
- *A3.8.2 – that are customary or usual; or*
- *A3.8.3 – that can reasonably be expected to occur and are not the result of the user or some third party being grossly negligent or acting in bad faith."*

▶ The one thing the General Safety Requirement (GSR) does not require is evidence of safety! It amounts to doublespeak and means the opposite of what it says. The proposed prohibition against the supply of products that "can reasonably be foreseen to cause injury" is extraordinarily vague. It may be open to constitutional challenge under the Charter of Rights and Freedoms on the grounds that potential suppliers have not been given sufficient notice of how to alter their conduct to avoid this prohibition.

▶ The GSR will be defined by "*the guiding principles on risk decision-making described above.*" Any product that *seems* reasonably safe, with "acceptable levels" or an "acceptable daily intake" of toxic chemicals or is declared "substantially equivalent" to traditional plant varieties, will be permitted to enter the food supply. If problems occur, they will be dealt with *after* the damage is done. The type of damage we are talking about affects the immune and reproduction systems of children and future generations not yet born. The GSR, in effect, places risk before safety, and is therefore incompatible with the Precautionary Principle.

▶ This approach requires no precautionary or preventative measures, no safety inspections, pre-market testing for safety or labelling. Under a GSR, the standard for food safety, for example, translates as "safe enough to be acceptable," leaving plenty of room to avoid liability. *Under the rules of a GSR, there is literally no limit to what the food industry would have us swallow.*

WHAT IT *REALLY* MEANS:

▶ The enactment of this GSR proposal will, in fact, further erode the regulatory obligations covering hazardous products in Canada. Industry lobbyists would pressure government for the adoption of, or recognition of, industry product standards and thus provide a safe haven against criminal liability under the GSR prohibition.

▸ The GSR is central to the shift from regulatory regimes to reliance on industry to self-regulate. The 2001 Report of the Auditor-General expressed concerns that public health and safety could be compromised by this policy because industry is known to place profit ahead of public health and safety. *http://www.oag-bvg.ca/domino/reports.nsf/html/0024ce.html (par. 29 and 30)*. A Health Canada study on the GSR that found the need of a company to maintain consumer confidence and avoid lawsuits "does not cause manufacturers to adopt measures to avoid injuries, where the cost of the measure is greater than the cost of settling civil actions for an injury or death." *http://www.healthcoalition.ca/tort-paper.pdf*

QUESTIONS

6.1 Why is Health Canada not enforcing the current provisions of the *Food & Drugs Act* requiring a manufacturer to demonstrate product safety before it is approved?

6.2 Why is the GSR – instead of the Precautionary Principle – the centrepiece of the new health protection proposal?

6.3 How does the public get a higher level of health protection from a lower standard of safety?

6.4 Why is Health Canada proposing a GSR, when a study it commissioned on the matter concluded that a GSR was not in the public interest?

6.5 Is the GSR Health Canada's attempt at "smart" regulation?

6.6 Would the adoption of the GSR, as proposed, make it illegal to manufacture or market meat infected with E-Coli (Hamburger Disease)?

CHAPTER 7

Transparency of the Review Process

WHAT HEALTH CANADA *SAYS*

"A number of provisions would have implications with regard to the evaluation of products by Health Canada. For example, the proposed Act would:
- *endorse the concept of transparency and public involvement in government decision-making;*
- *reinforce the authority of Health Canada to collect, use and disclose information in the public interest, while establishing a code of conduct to protect the confidentiality of personal and commercial information;* [the current broad definition of commercial confidentiality is the key problem]
- *allow Health Canada to inform the public of enforcement actions taken under the Act, including inspection reports, subject to protecting confidential information..."*

(**Detailed Legislative Proposal**, p.55)

REALITY CHECK

▸ Health Canada's proposals give the impression that transparency, making information on product approvals public, and public involvement are all goals that current health protection legislation prohibits or discourages.

Let them eat Prozac!

"The Prozac-and-suicide saga reveals a structural problem in the system that gives us drugs, biotechnology, and other health care products. And this structural problem, this fault line, is highly likely to produce a drug or health care disaster at least equivalent to that of thalidomide on the Richter scale of drug disasters. And very soon." –Dr. David Healy.

Healy shows that some of the patients taking Prozac, Paxil and Zoloft can become suicidal and commit suicide at a much higher rate than if they had been left untreated. The manufacturers have refused to acknowledge this risk, key national regulators have not taken appropriate steps to protect the safety of their citizens, and critics of these drugs have been harassed and threatened.

"There is no nice way of putting this: The drug companies have sub-ordinated patient safety on the altar of blockbuster profits. Aggressive marketing has persuaded the medical profession to prescribe [these] drugs to people who are simply struggling with mundane anxieties. Unwilling to risk the death of a goose that lays such golden eggs, the companies refuse to sponsor the kind of large-scale scientific research that would map out the true frequency and seriousness of side-effects."

–Arthur Schafer, *Globe & Mail*, Books, October 18, 2003, p. D8.

David Healy, *Let Them Eat Prozac*, Toronto: Lorimer, 2003 (*http://www.healyprozac.com*)

▶ Excessive secrecy combined with the failure to enforce the *Food & Drugs Act* is the problem with Health Canada's drug approval process. The current legislative proposal will not improve this situation.

Big Pharma's Role

"Their role [the pharmaceutical industry's] has changed from developing the drugs that society really needs to trying to extract as much money as they possibly can from the health care system."

–Arnold Relman, MD, Professor Emeritus, Harvard Medical School (*Financial Times of London*, Oct. 24, 2003).

▸ If Health Canada was performing its legal duty to protect public health and safety, there would be no need to hide the information upon which products are approved. All it takes is a Minister of Health who is willing to perform his legal duty.

WHAT IT *REALLY* MEANS

▸ The proposals on the transparency of the drug approval process cover up the real issues. Secrecy in drug regulation at Health Canada far exceeds legal obligations and the "duty of care." Excessive secrecy in the Therapeutic Products Directorate means: a) proper accountability is impossible, b) vulnerability to industrial capture and collusion between regulator and the regulated, and c) industry's scientific experts have extensive conflicts of interest while providing their expert advice.

▸ Even the Minister of Health's Science Advisory Board showed that the current excessive level of secrecy in not legally required. (*http://www.hc-sc.gc.ca/sab-ccs/report_drp_e.html#62*) Currently, reports on studies of the safety and effectiveness of new drugs that are considered commercially confidential in Canada are freely available on the U.S. Food and Drug Administration's web-site. These are the same companies, the same products, and the same safety and effectiveness studies as those considered to be secret here. The reason is that we define "commercial confidentiality" in an excessively broad manner. It has nothing to do with what's in the law.

▶ While Health Canada consults on a shopping list of external recommendations it has no intention of acting on, other initiatives are underway. Real change is happening elsewhere. For example, the 2002 *Speech From The Throne* announced a "Smart Regulation Strategy" that would "contribute to innovation and economic growth, and to reduce the administrative burden on business." These policy initiatives will make sure Health Canada's drug regulator remains incapable of delivering publicly defensible assessments, which are uncompromisingly in the interests of public health. As long as the policy is to put industry profits ahead of health and safety, secrecy will reign.

▶ The 2002 *Speech from the Throne* also announced: *"As part of this strategy, the government will adapt its intellectual property framework to enable Canada to be a world leader on emerging issues such as new life-forms. It will speed up the regulatory process for drug approvals to ensure that Canadians have faster access to the safe drugs they need, creating a better climate for research in pharmaceuticals."*

QUESTIONS

7.1 Why does Health Canada keep secret the information upon which it based its decision to approve a product? Why should Canadians trust a culture of secrecy that risks lives?

7.2 Why does Health Canada have transparency and openness in the regulatory process for *industry* (e.g., making and bending the rules; self-regulatory regimes; standards development) but resists transparency and openness *for the public* (e.g., information on the safety of products)? Who is Health Canada's client?

7.3 Why is Health Canada not monitoring adverse drug reactions and keeping data on the number of injuries and deaths occurring each year in Canada as a result of medicine use?

7.4 What evidence does Health Canada have that a speedier drug approval process would lead to health benefits for Canadians, given the lack of evidence of therapeutic advantage for most new drugs, and the serious potential for harm when new drugs are found to have unexpected harmful effects?

7.5 Given the evidence from the Women's Health Initiative trial that the prescribing of hormone replacement therapy for disease prevention is likely to have led to unnecessary heart attacks, strokes, potentially fatal blood clots, breast cancer and dementia among the millions of Canadian women prescribed this therapy, and the evidence from the ALLHAT trial of unnecessary strokes and heart attacks among the millions of Canadians prescribed newer anti-hypertensives rather than more effective older thera-

Health Canada's Recipe For
Public Consultation on Pharmaceutical
Issues: 1/3rd drug industry representatives;

1/3rd health professionals funded by drug industry

1/3rd patient and disease groups funded by drug industry

+ a couple of disinterested participants for "balance."

pies, why is Health Canada not changing the drug approval process to require evidence of a therapeutic advantage, in terms of true health outcomes, for new drugs?

7.6 Why is Health Canada aiming to speed up the drug approval process when more than 90% of new drugs do not offer any significant therapeutic benefit over existing drugs?

7.7 Why is Health Canada not strengthening its examination of the information submitted by drug companies in the approval process, since research has shown that, when drug companies sponsor studies, they are more than four times as likely to show positive results than when funding comes from other sources?

Conflict of Interest + Secrecy ≠ "Science-Based" Regulation

"If the same government agency that is charged with the responsibility to protect the public health and environmental safety from risks posed by technologies also is charged with the promotion of that same technology, and if its safety assessments are, by official policy, balanced against the economic interests of the industries that develop them, this represents, from the point of view of both the public and the individual stakeholders, a significant conflict of interest. Each stakeholder is placed in the position of having to ask, with respect to each regulatory decision, whether its own interests have been unduly compromised by the interests of the other...

"The claim that the assessment of biotechnology risks is "science-based" is only as valid as the independence, objectivity, and quality of the science employed...The more the regulatory agencies are, or are perceived to be, promoters of the technology, the more they undermine public trust in their ability to regulate the technology in the public interest.

"The amount of information the regulatory departments choose to disclose from the application and approval process is not set by any formal regulations. Rather, it is a policy judgment that seeks to balance the interests of industry against the desire for transparency in the regulatory process.

"The conflict of interest involved in both promoting and regulating an industry or technology is also a factor in the issue of transparency, and therefore the scientific integrity of the regulatory process. In effect, the public interest in a regulatory system that is "science-based" – that meets the scientific standards of objectivity, a major aspect of which is full openness to scientific peer review – is significantly compromised when that openness is negotiated away by regulators in exchange for cordial and supportive relationships with the industries being regulated.

"In the judgment of the Expert Panel, the more regulatory agencies limit free access to the data upon which their decisions are based, the more compromised becomes the claim that the regulatory process is "science-based." This is due to a simple but well-understood requirement of the scientific method itself – that it be an open, completely transparent enterprise in which any and all aspects of scientific research are open to full review by scientific peers. Peer review and independent corroboration of research findings are axioms of the scientific method, and part of the very meaning of the objectivity and neutrality of science."

–Royal Society of Canada, *Elements of Precaution: Recommendations for the Regulation of Food Biotechnology in Canada*, (*http://rsc.ca/foodbiotechnology/GMreportEN.pdf*) p. 212-214.

CHAPTER 8

Review of Novel Products (Genetically Modified Food)

WHAT HEALTH CANADA *SAYS*

"With respect to genetically modified food, the recommendations [of the Expert Panel on the Future of Food Biotechnology of the Royal Society of Canada http://rsc.ca/foodbiotechnology/ GMreportEN.pdf] *which are of particular interest to the renewal of the health protection legislation include the following:*

- *• 9.2 The panel recommends that the Canadian regulatory agencies seek ways to increase the public transparency of the scientific data and scientific rationales upon which their decisions are based."*

(**Detailed Legislative Proposal**, p. 59)

REALITY CHECK

▶ Several years after genetically modified (GM) food was mixed into 75% of all Canadian processed food, Health Canada asked an Expert Panel of the Royal Society (RSC) to evaluate its safety. The Panel found that Canadians are not being adequately protected from the risks of genetically modified foods and other biotech products. The safety of GM food has never been established by science. The RSC said the biotechnology industry must demonstrate the safety of a product *before* it can be approved. The expert panel called for the immediate application of the Precautionary Principle in the regulation of food biotechnology **under the existing legislative and regulatory framework**. Health Canada questioned the "factual validity" of the Panel and refused to act on any of its key recommendations.

▸ The Expert Panel report says: *"New technologies should not be presumed safe unless there is a reliable scientific basis for considering them safe. The Panel rejects the use of 'substantial equivalence' as a decision threshold to exempt new GM products from rigorous safety assessments on the basis of superficial similarities because such a regulatory procedure is not a precautionary assignment of the burden of proof"...."The Panel finds the use of 'substantial equivalence' to exempt GM products from rigorous scientific assessment **to be scientifically unjustifiable and inconsistent with precautionary regulation of the technology**."* (Emphasis added.)

▸ European Union policy is to accompany life sciences research with research on safety aspects of the new technology generated. The Government of Canada conducts no research on the safety of biotechnology. According to a senior Industry Canada official, testing for safety would be "counter-productive" in light of the government's "see-no-evil" biotechnology policy. Health Canada has all but eliminated its capacity for independent scientific research on product safety. The policy is to leave this responsibility to industry. The fox has been put in charge of the chicken coup. But Canada still had the audacity to take the EU to court over the moratorium it imposed on GMOs. The Canadian Trade Minister claimed the EU moratorium was not consistent with the WTO because it was "not based on scientific risk assessment!" Having force-fed Canadians untested GM food, the Government of Canada attempted, outrageously, to force European governments to expose their own citizens to the same risks. Unbelievable.

▸ Dr. Arpad Pusztai studied the effects of GM potatoes on rats in the U.K. After only 10 days, the rats developed "significant changes to their vital organs," including abnormal stimulation of the pancreas, intestine, prostate and testicles, liver atrophy, and weakened heart. He also observed a startling genetic instability in the potato. Within two days of making these findings known, he was fired, his scientific research team disbanded, the lab closed, and all data confiscated. So much for scientific rigor in establishing the safety of GM food! (*http://www.healthcoalition. ca/pusztai.html*).

▸ Without a scientific risk assessment there can be no risk management to estimate the probable harm to persons and environments. In chemistry, there is a science called toxicology which allows one to judge some risk. In biotechnology, there is no comparable science to assess risk of releasing live genetic organisms into the environment and into the food supply. In the absence of both science and risk management, Health Canada cannot regulate food biotechnology. Instead, the Government of Canada promotes food biotechnology using the dubious expertise of the public relations industry.

▸ The RSC Report found excessive secrecy among federal regulators about biotech safety, and criticized the cozy relationship between regulators and the biotech industry. The panel also said the co-opting of biotechnology science in universities by commercial interests and the emphasis on secrecy contributes to the general erosion of public confidence in the objectivity and independence of the science behind the regulation of food biotechnology.

▸ In effect, Canada's health protection system, like Canada's current food supply, is rigged to deceive. You are what you eat, but government and industry won't let you know what that is. A major function of the secrecy in Health Canada's regulatory system is to prevent accountability and public examination of regulatory decisions. If vital risk assessment data are kept secret – in some cases even kept from the scientists doing the product review – how can the public know there is in fact a valid and not a fraudulent scientific assessment? (*http://www.healthcoalition.cu/ whistleblowers.html, http://www.parl.gc.ca/36/1/parlbus/commbus/ senate/com-e/agri-e/rep-e/repintermar99-e.htm*)

▸ The current proposal on "novel food" selects a few Royal Society recommendations out of context and diverts attention away from the central point: Health Canada's refusal to adopt the Precautionary Principle – at great risk to health, safety, and the environment, and arguably in contravention of the law. The *Canadian Environmental Protection Act* states that, under the Constitution and the laws of Canada, the government must apply "the precautionary principle...Where there are threats of serious or irreversible damage, lack of full scientific certainty shall not be used as reason for postponing cost-effective measures to prevent environmental degradation."

▸ The "novel food" proposals shift the burden of proof placed on the manufacturer in the *Food & Drugs Act* to demonstrate product safety onto the public to demonstrate proof of harm. The potential harm we are talking about with genetically modified food is unknown, unobservable, and uncontrollable (*See Chart 2*).

▸ Assuming "novel products" are safe until proven otherwise may lead to "soft disasters" – large-scale health and environmental problems that emerge slowly but at high cost to society. Such disasters mostly occur because excessive faith was placed in limited or flawed data about the safety of a product or technology, ignoring possible eventualities where there is little or no information, and unintended effects.

▸ The history of Mad Cow disease (BSE) offers a chilling warning of the unpredictable dangers inherent in tampering with nature and biology. Biological boundaries are real and DNA is not just "information" that can be freely passed from one species to another with impunity. Mad Cow disease happened when, for economic reasons, herbivores were fed rendered animal parts derived from other species, something they would never eat in nature. Commercial interests forced the crossing of biological boundaries, resulting in a terrible new disease. Feeding rendered animal protein back to cattle does not compare with the com-

GM "could be another Thalidomide"

"The Agricultural Insurance Underwriters Agency, owned by Norwich Union/Sun Alliance and Rural Insurance Group run by Lloyds, refuse to insure GM crops in the U.K. "When insurers qualify GM crops in the same category as Thalidomide, asbestos and terrorism, no thinking farmer should risk their business by taking unproven, unwanted and unnecessary technology."

–*UK Evening Standard*, 7 October 2003 (*www.thisislondon. com/news/articles*)

plexity and scope of changes introduced in our diet through GM food.

QUESTIONS

8.1 What do Canadians think of the fact that Health Canada is willing to "trade off" potential adverse and irreversible effects to health and the environment in order to promote biotechnology in "novel" food and drugs?

8.2 When did Health Canada's policy change from health protection to promoting the "risk-benefits" of biotechnology in food and drugs? What is the legal basis for this policy that abandons the "duty of care" for health and safety?

8.3 Why did Health Canada ignore the Royal Society's Expert Panel Report: *Elements of Precaution* and the recommendation to immediately adopt the Precautionary Principle as the basis for regulating food biotechnology?

8.4 If Health Canada's approval of GM food is science-based, where is the science?

8.5 When did the Canadian people or Parliament debate the benefits and risks of biotechnology in general and genetically modified food in particular?

8.6 Since 97% of Canadians want GM food labelled, why does Health Canada prevent mandatory labelling?

INFACT Canada
Infant Feeding Action Coalition

6 Trinity Square Toronto ON M5G 1B1 • Phone: (416) 595 - 9819 • Fax: (416) 591 - 9355 • infoc@infactcanada.ca • www.infactcanada.ca

October 29, 2003

Michael McBane
Canadian Health Coalition

Re: Risk First, Safety Last!

Dear Mike,

What scares me about Health Canada s proposal is that there is not even a mandate for education or warnings about risks for those who are affected by the lack of regulation and monitoring. In fact my experience is that there is a concerted effort by Health Canada to avoid any communication to the public about the risks either as health warnings or on labels.

In the area of infant foods the warnings have been to protect industry interests rather than the public need to know. For example, powdered infant formulas are not sterile and several deaths have been reported in the literature when these products were contaminated by pathogens. Health Canada's response was to issue a health warning to hospitals to make sure they prepared the formulas according to the manufacturers instructions (perhaps to safeguard against).

I have repeatedly asked Health Canada to issue the same warning to the public/expectant and new parents as there is a perception that these products are sterile, but they have refused. Also INFACT Canada has repeatedly asked for label changes to warn about potential contaminants and to warn about proper preparation again no. However the industry is permitted to put the preparation instructions on the inside of the label and a parent has to peel off the label to read the very difficult blue print on the inside. The outside of the label is of course used to make misleading health claims for the product. Both of these violate the Food and Drugs Act.

On the question of Novel food, the short-term health and safety effects of GM foods/Novel Foods are difficult to assess. Cause and effect between foods consumed and health outcomes are extremely difficult to determine and the subtle or long-term effects will likely not be known until years later. So the industry can make claims and do as they please as we all participate in the unregulated and unmonitored mass human trials. Also all animal studies have to exhaustively determine safety before human trials are conducted at least that s what the ethicists say& And of course we have the test of time that conventionally produced foods (other than chemical inputs and contaminants) will ensure optimal growth, development, health and environmental protection. The risk analysis comes out at the wrong end here.

The term "Novel" food should be considered a misnomer as it does not define the method of production. It is a marketing term and not a scientific term.

Sincerely,

Elizabeth Sterken

Elizabeth Sterken, Nutritionist
Executive Director, INFACT Canada

CHAPTER 9

Direct-to-Consumer Drug Advertising

WHAT HEALTH CANADA *SAYS*

"When adopting new regulations, some of the tools to be considered in designing an appropriate scheme could include one or a combination of the following: (pp.86-92)
Option 1 – Prohibiting advertising for prescription drugs
Option 2 – Not impose any restrictions on advertising
Option 3 – Allow advertising but establish general criteria..."

The *Detailed Legislative Proposal* argues against Option 1 – the status quo; presents three pro and three con arguments for Option 2 – letting industry do what it wants; and presents 12 pro arguments for Option 3 – "general criteria" so industry can self-regulate and do what it wants.

REALITY CHECK

▶ According to a recent editorial in the Canadian Medical Association Journal (*http://www.cmaj.ca/cgi/reprint/169/5/381.pdf*), the purpose of direct-to-consumer advertising (DTCA) is to create demand by delivering a double message of anxiety and hope, encouraging a belief that a condition – hair loss, acne, shyness, allergies – is not only widespread and serious, but "treatable." Ads create new and often undesirable market niches. Drug ads are not about educating patients. The ads promote the use of newer, more expensive drugs (even if older and cheaper ones work as well or better) and increase brand recognition. Drug companies want DTCA to boost drug sales and profits.

▶ DTCA would add millions of dollars to the cost of Medicare. There are many health concerns and no known health benefits. The public resources that would go to drug company profits would be better spent in providing unbiased information about drugs and alternative non-drug therapies and prevention.

QUESTION

9.1 When all the evidence shows that DTCA is not in the public interest and will have a negative impact on health policy, drug insurance plans, and public health, why is Health Canada even discussing this industry proposal?

Notes on Key Terms

RISK; RISK SOCIETY; RISK ASSESSMENT; RISK
MANAGEMENT; PRECAUTIONARY PRINCIPLE; SCIENCE;
"SOUND SCIENCE"; SUBSTANTIAL EQUIVALENCE; AND
GM FOOD.

RISK

The word appears to have been first coined by 16th or 17th century
European explorers to refer to sailing into uncharted waters. The
notion of risk is a social construct of modern industrial civiliza-
tion. Traditional cultures didn't have a concept of risk because
they didn't need one. Traditional cultures did not see the future
or nature as something to be conquered. The concept of "risk" and
"risk assessment" emerged at the centre of policy debate about
technology, environment, and society in the late 1960s and early
1970s in the U.S.

Risk does not refer to hazard or danger. Risk refers to hazards
that are actively assessed in relation to future possibilities or
benefits. Risk presupposes decision-making about what hazards
are acceptable. In today's corporate power game of risk, technical experts, often working under the patronage of industry, define agendas and impose premises on risk discourse. Knowledge

about risk, just as the perception of risk, depends on contextual factors ranging from individual or organizational experience to political culture and global corporate power.

What people claim to know about risk is in fact constructed in different ways in different political and cultural settings. Canada and the European Union, for example, differ fundamentally on issues of risk, health risk assessment, and the application of the Precautionary Principle to products like asbestos, growth hormones in meat, and genetically modified organisms in food. Canada's economic strategy for the 21st century is to create global trade in risk and biohazards (untested, unlabeled, uninsurable, and uncontrollable).

Along with today's growing capacity of technical options grows the incalculability of their consequences. The hazards of genetic engineering technology, for example, abolish the foundations and categories according to which we have thought and acted to this point. In aggressively promoting biotechnology with its unknown and unintended consequences, Canada has become a negative international leader in promoting risk. Canada is also a leader in resisting the application of the Precautionary Principle. This can be described as a form of "organized irresponsibility." The decisions are so impersonal and well hidden from public scrutiny and accountability as to have no responsibilities for the potentially deadly consequences.

RISK SOCIETY

A concept developed by German sociologist Ulrich Beck. It describes a situation in which the social, political, ecological, and individual risks created by the momentum of innovation increasingly elude the control and protective institutions of industrial society. In risk society, the new hazards being produced (e.g. nuclear power, genetic engineering, zenotransplantation, gene therapy) undermine or cancel the established safety systems of traditional risk calculations. Nuclear, chemical, ecological, and genetic engineering risks, in contrast to earlier industrial risks, a) cannot be limited in time or place, b) are not accountable to established rules of blame, liability, or causality, and c) cannot be compensated or insured against. To express this in a single example: the injured of Chernobyl are today, many years after the catastrophe, not even all *born* yet.

RISK ASSESSEMENT

Industry and government decision-makers generally decide what they want to do, and instead of examining all the alternatives, they hire a scientist or risk assessor to convince everyone that the damage they are about to do to us is "acceptable." In order to decide what the "risk" of a given negative event is, risk assessors make a series of assumptions about the context in which it arises. **Current approaches to risk assessment, especially in the field of biotechnology in Canada, fail to recognize that the underlying assumptions used in the process of risk assessment affect the outcome.** Risk assessment is driven by assumptions, not by science. As a rule: garbage in, garbage out. When Canadian Ministers of Health, Agriculture, and International Trade claim that the regulation of biotechnology products is not based on assumptions or judgments, but solely on "sound science," they illustrate Lonergan's "principle of the empty head." In fact, profound ignorance of the scientific process appears to be a characteristic of current Ministers of the Crown.

The kind of imagination risk assessors bring to their activity depends on their objectives, values, training, bias, and experience. The models conventionally used in Canada and the U.S by analysts to assess risks to public health reflect deep-seated biases and basic omissions. One example: the "discovery" in recent years that vulnerable populations – women, children, the elderly, Aboriginal people and ethnic minorities – have been systematically underrepresented in scientific inquiries concerning health risks (e.g., DES, pesticides) and common diseases in North America. Gender and ethnic bias, and insensitivity to children's exposure, can never be justified as legitimate exercises in science policy or regulation. The public understanding of risk and hazards is much greater than that of the "experts" and reflects legitimate concerns that are typically omitted from "expert" risk assessments. Risk assessors who don't look for harmful effects – and therefore don't find any – engage in what is sometimes called "take-the-money-and-run toxicology."

RISK MANAGEMENT

Risk management is the decision-making process involving considerations of political, social, economic and engineering factors. Pursuant to relevant risk assessments relating to the potential hazard, regulatory options are developed to select a response to risk. In effect, risk management involves the decision as to how many people will be permitted to become ill or die. The law of environmental risk is that pollution follows the poor. This approach displaces the public health model, which uses a much higher standard of safety: the Precautionary Principle. Instead of managing deadly risks, the goal is to protect health and prevent the damage from occurring in the first place. Risk management (or risk-benefit management) is key to the Government of Canada's economic objective of promoting biotechnology as an "economic engine." The current approach to the regulation of biotechnology in Canada – risk management without the Precautionary Principle – is like playing a game of Russian roulette without knowing the odds.

In light of the enormous scientific ignorance in the senior management ranks of federal regulatory agencies, especially Health Canada and the Canadian Food Inspection Agency, it may be that Canada's regulatory system is actually incapable of conducting risk management. Instead, Health Canada senior management is actually engaged in risk *issue* management. Managers have adopted science with "spin." This explains why safety research scientists and their budgets are cut and replaced with communications and administrative personnel, and industry public relations consultants. The so-called science-based regulators have less and less science, and more and more industry information and propaganda.

PRECAUTIONARY PRINCIPLE

According to the Royal Society of Canada's Expert Panel on Food Biotechnology, it is "a regulatory mechanism for managing environmental and health risk arising from incomplete scientific knowledge of a proposed activity's or technology's impact." "The Precautionary Principle has its roots in a sense of skepticism about the ability of science, or any system of knowledge, to understand and predict fully the function of complex biological and ecological systems. The Principle is essentially about how to manage risks when one does not have fully reliable knowledge about the identity, character, or magnitude of those risks. It assumes that there is often the possibility of error in the assessment of risks, and the higher the potential for this error, the greater the precaution it prescribes in proceeding with actions that place certain values at risk." (*Royal Society of Canada's Expert Panel on Food Biotechnology*, p 197.) *See Appendix 1.*

The *Canadian Environmental Protection Act* states that, under the Constitution and the laws of Canada, the government must apply "the precautionary principle...Where there are threats of serious or irreversible damage, lack of full scientific certainty shall not be used as reason for postponing cost-effective measures to prevent environmental degradation." The Precautionary Principle deliberately shifts the burden of proof onto the party in favour of a potentially risky course of action. And where there is the possibility of irreversible damage to natural life-support functions, precautionary action should be taken *irrespective of the forgone benefits.*

The Principle emerged in a world where the calculation of risk, as it has been established so far by science and legal institutions, has collapsed. Along with the growing capacity of technical options grows the incalculability of their consequences. The private insurance industry – perhaps the greatest symbol of calculation and alternative security – does not cover genetic engineering, nuclear disaster, or climate change. The risks produced today completely evade human perceptive abilities, produce systemic and often irreversible harm, and endanger *all* forms of life on this planet.

According to the European Commission: "Whether or not to invoke the Precautionary Principle is a decision exercised where scientific information is insufficient, inconclusive, or uncertain, and where there are indications that the possible effects on the environment or human, animal or plant health may be potentially dangerous and inconsistent with the chosen level of protection... The appropriate response in a given situation is thus the result of a political decision, a function of the risk level that is "acceptable" to the society on which the risk is imposed." (*Communication from the Commission on the Precautionary Principle*, 2000).

Online: *www.eurpoa.eu.int/comm/dgs/health_consumer/library/pub/pub07_en.pdf.*

Health Canada is concerned that the precautionary principle is a challenge to science-based regulation and to the allocation of resources based on risk assessment. The Royal Society of Canada Expert Panel has established the fact that there is no "science-based" regulation in Canada of food biotechnology, for example. We have also seen the problem with risk assessment being delegated to industry or industry-friendly risk assessors. There appears to be no concern for these problems by senior managers at Health Canada.

SCIENCE

Science is conventionally held to imply a series of key properties, including a systematic methodology, skepticism, transparency, quality control by peer-review, professional independence and accountability, and open to continual change in the face of learning. If a risk assessment is secret and relies solely on industry research that is not peer-reviewed, you are not dealing with science any more. Health Canada's current system of regulation for food, drugs, and medical devices has the opposite characteristics of science. Health Canada food, drug, and biotechnology regulation is secret, unaccountable, ad hoc, ridden with conflict of interest, narrow, doctrinaire, and captured by corporate interests. Health Canada scientists who adhere to the conventional norms of science and attempt to enforce the *Food & Drugs Act* are gagged, disciplined, and threatened by senior management and industry.

(**http://www.parl.gc.ca/36/1/parlbus/commbus/senate/com-e/agri-e/rep-e/repintermar99-e.htm**)

Health Canada's new Office of Chief Scientist is headed by an entrepreneur with commercial interests in a biotechnology company. His job requirements include: "willing to take risks," but not willing to apply the Precautionary Principle.

"SOUND SCIENCE"

A term used by U.S. and Canadian government regulators, politicians, industry officials, and industry-funded scientists. It operates as an ideology, pre-empting debate on the framing of scientific uncertainty. According to this ideology, only evidence that is supportive of biotechnology is scientifically defensible. Anything not supportive is, by definition, unsound. **The policy of relying on claims of "sound science" is itself unsound.** Science is ill-equipped to deal with the societal, ethical, and environmental ramifications of biotechnology. Scientists are under pressure to reach definitive conclusions on risk when none can be definitively established. Biotechnology is characterized by significant scientific ignorance and uncertainties, as well as absence of critical information, and the narrow scope of the questions researched. Canada claims its regulation of GM food is science-based. But it uses the unscientific and ill-defined concept of "substantial equivalence" in order to exempt GM products from rigorous scientific risk assessment for toxicity. Canada's regulation of GM food is, according to the Royal Society of Canada's Expert Panel, "scientifically unjustifiable."

When Health Canada and the CFIA use the term "sound science," it is doublespeak – intended to deceive and confuse. Health Canada now relies on the industries it regulates to provide the "science" on a product submission. For example, when the chemical giant Monsanto says what its secret science means, that is what Health Canada says the science is. But the public can't review the "science" because it is a secret. Monsanto's problem at Health Canada began when the scientist reviewing its rBGH (bovine growth hormone) submission exposed the fact that Monsanto failed to provide data on toxicity to human health. In other words, "sound science" may be used as a cover for no science.

(http://www.parl.gc.ca/36/1/parlbus/commbus/senate/
com-e/agri-e/rep-e/repintermar99-e.htm)
The regulatory role of science depends upon various political
and economic influences. Risk regulation using "sound science"
makes subjective judgments about what must be protected, what
uncertainties matter for risk assessment, what research is needed
to clarify them, and what counts as meaningful evidence. The use
of the term "sound science" is intended to conceal and restrict
the economic, political, and ethical judgments, while the Precautionary Principle has tended to reveal the assumptions for examination and democratic policy debate. The Precautionary Principle
is not less "objective" than "sound science." In fact, a strong case
can be made that a precautionary methodology is *more* "scientific."

SUBSTANTIAL EQUIVALENCE

This concept, according to the OECD, "embodies the idea that existing organisms used as foods, or as a source of food, can be used
as the basis for comparison when assessing the safety of human
consumption of a food or food component that has been genetically engineered or modified." Making "substantial equivalence"
the basis of science-based regulation of GM food is preposterous;
first, because it has never been properly defined in science or in
legislation; and second, because the degree of difference between
a natural food and its GM alternative before its "substance" ceases to be acceptably "equivalent" is also undefined. As pointed out
by Millstone and colleagues: "It is exactly this vagueness which
makes the concept useful to industry, but unacceptable to the
consumer." (*Nature*, 7 October 1999.)

Scientists working for the GM food companies and their "partners" in promotion at Health Canada and the CFIA claim an "absence of evidence" of harm to human health (without looking for
any) and then conclude that this demonstrates "evidence of absence" of risk to human health. As a basis for regulating GM food,
it is "scientifically unjustifiable" (*RSC Expert Panel*, 2001). When
combined with the absolute secrecy of the Health Canada and
CFIA regulatory regime, substantial equivalence creates the con-

ditions for corporate fraud. No wonder the Canadian public has come to mistrust Canada's "scientific" approach to GM food.

GM FOOD

Food that has been genetically modified; an organism into whose genome has been deliberately inserted one or more pieces of new DNA (deoxyribonucleic acid – the molecule that encodes genetic information). Recombinant DNA technology is an inherently risky method for producing new foods. Its risks are in large part due to the complexity and interdependence of the parts of the living system, including its DNA. Because of this complexity and interactivity of living systems – and because of the extent to which our understanding of them is very limited – it is impossible to predict what specific problems could result in the case of any particular genetically engineered organism. Mad Cow disease should serve as a warning that crossing biological barriers to generate higher profits can result in unpredictable dangers. Imagine the risks inherent in tampering with the genetic blueprint of life and then commercializing the technology in unlabelled food.

Dr. Arpad Pusztai of the Royal Society of Edinburgh was fired and his research confiscated when he found negative effects of GM potatoes on laboratory rats. There have been no properly controlled clinical trials looking at the effects of short- or long-term ingestion of GM foods by humans. "We are eating things which we have not eaten before," said Dr. Pusztai, "and I challenge anyone who can predict the consequences of this. Particularly for our immune system, which is there to protect us from injury coming from the outside world. People feel very concerned about their food, not just for their sake, but for the sake of their children and grandchildren".
(http://pdf.thelancet.com/pdfdownload?uid=llan.354.9187. original_research.2945.1&x=x.pdf).

GM food has a history of misrepresentation and suppression of scientific evidence. Key experiments were not performed, or were performed badly and then misrepresented.

Private insurance companies establish the frontier barrier of risk society. Genetic engineering, a new danger industry, is not insurable. Risk society is sailing into uncharted waters, beyond the insurance limit. What do insurance underwriters know about GM food that Health Canada and the food industry aren't telling us? If the food is safe and more advantageous, why are regulators and manufacturers preventing consumers from knowing what they are eating by having informative labels on products containing genetically modified organisms? If there is zero risk, why is there no insurance coverage?

Ten Myths of Direct-to-Consumer Drug Advertising

BY BARBARA MINTZES, CENTRE FOR HEALTH SERVICES AND POLICY RESEARCH, UBC

MYTH 1

DTC advertising educates and empowers patients.

Reality check: By definition, advertising aims to sell a product, and cannot provide the impartial unbiased information patients need for shared informed treatment choices. A 10-year review of over 300 print ads in major U.S. magazines found that most ads failed to provide key educational information needed by patients. For example, nine out of 10 did not say how likely a drug is to work, and most made no mention of any other treatment. From 1997 and 2001, over 90 DTC ad campaigns were found to violate U.S. law, mainly because of inadequate risk information and exaggerated benefits. Repeat violations were frequent. This is hardly patient empowerment.

MYTH 2

DTC ads inform the public about available treatments.

Reality check: Only a small subset of medicines is advertised to the public. Consistently, 40% of annual spending is on 10 brands. These are mainly new, expensive drugs for long-term use by large target audiences. Off-patent drugs are never advertised, even if they the first choice for treatment, such as thiazide diuretics for high blood pressure. To get a new drug to market, a company does not need to show it is any better than existing alternatives, and most new drugs offer little to no therapeutic advantage. The Patented Medicines Pricing Review Board judged only 6% of 415 new drugs introduced from 1996-2000 to be breakthroughs.

MYTH 3

Only the safest medicines are advertised to the public.

Reality check: In the U.S., drugs that were later withdrawn for safety reasons have been advertised to the public, including troglitazone (Rezulin), a diabetes drug named as the suspected cause in nearly 400 deaths. In Canada, Diane-35, a second-line acne treatment, has been heavily advertised to the public in spite of safety advisories showing a higher risk of potentially fatal blood clots than other similar hormonal products. DTC advertising promotes the rapid widespread use of new medicines, when relatively little is known about their less common or longer-term risks. Imagine another thalidomide or DES with the extra boost of DTC advertising.

MYTH 4

DTC ads lead to better health because people seek treatment Earlier.

Reality check: Ads can bring patients to their doctors' offices, but some of the most dramatic examples are for conditions like toenail fungus. The hypothesis that ads bring in those likely to benefit from drug treatment to a greater extent than those unlikely to benefit has not been tested. There is both broad under- and over-treatment of many medical conditions, and many ad campaigns cast a wide net, focusing on mild symptoms rather than serious disease.

MYTH 5

Since a prescription is needed, the patient is protected.

Reality check: A survey in doctors' offices, published in the Canadian Medical Association Journal in September 2003, found that, when patients asked for a specific brand of drug, three times out of four the doctor obliged by prescribing it – often in spite of ambivalence about the choice of treatment. This is consistent with reports of high prescribing rates in response to patient requests in the pharmaceutical marketing literature. DTCA puts doctors under pressure to prescribe advertised brands.

MYTH 6

Made-in-Canada ads would be more socially responsible than U.S. ads.

Reality check: The best example of what Canadian DTC ads may be like comes from New Zealand. Like Canada, New Zealand relies mainly on industry self-regulation of drug promotion, whereas the U.S. has direct government regulation. Every New Zealand ad I have seen would be illegal in the U.S., mainly because of the lack of risk information. In New Zealand, as in Canada, if a complaint is made about an ad, the arbitration process is slow and cumbersome, and ads continue to run while their legality is under discussion.

MYTH 7

In Canada, it is legal to advertise a prescription medicine to the public if you state the name, but not the approved use, or vice-versa.

Key recommendations on DTCA

There is an ongoing public health rationale for maintaining the existing prohibition of direct-to-consumer advertising of prescription drugs. However, we need to seriously examine whether our current approach to enforcement is consistent with health protection aims.

The Canadian public needs accurate, up-to-date, comparative information on available treatment options, both drug and non-drug, and on the conditions they treat. Production and distribution should be publicly financed as a necessary component of health care services, and should be fully independent of commercial interests.

Reality check: This interpretation of the law began to appear in Health Canada documents in late 2000. The cited basis is a 1978 price advertising amendment. This interpretation is consistent neither with the spirit of the law, nor its wording, nor with the underlying public health aims. The 1978 price advertising amendment explicitly prohibits any representations other than name, price and quantity, and these ads have many other representations, such as images, suggestions to ask your doctor, and so on.

MYTH 8

We must change the law because the current prohibition of DTC advertising would not stand up to a legal challenge.

Reality check: This assertion is based on a 1995 Supreme Court case on tobacco advertising, which found that Health Canada had not shown that a full ban on advertising met public health goals better than a partial ban. Since 1995, we have a new Tobacco Act, we don't have tobacco advertising, and the law has stood up to legal challenges up to the Quebec High Court level. The partial ban on prescription drug advertising is consistent with legal restrictions on sales: companies may advertise to health professionals, but not the public.

MYTH 9

Restrictions on advertising of prevention or cure of "serious diseases" such as Schedule A, were appropriate in 1953, but are a quaint anomaly in the 21st century.

Reality check: People who are seriously ill, or are trying to prevent future death and disability, are vulnerable in a way that someone who is going out to buy a new car is not. One has to look no farther than Pfizer's tagged-toe-of-a-corpse campaign to promote its cholesterol-lowering drug Lipitor. World Health Organization staff wrote a letter to the British journal *The Lancet* about this ad campaign, charging that it uses fear of death to sell a product, provides a misleading impression of cardiovascular risk, and is likely to induce medically unjustified drug use.

MYTH 10

Prescription drug advertising is highly regulated in Canada.

Reality check: In Canada, we rely primarily on industry self-regulation of drug promotion. We have no explicit requirements for balanced benefit and risk information. We do not actively monitor advertising, and most violations go unpunished and misinformation goes uncorrected. If a complaint is made, the ad is allowed to run until a decision is made. Why does this matter? Ask the 22-year-old UBC student who was hospitalized for a pulmonary embolism after taking Diane-35 for mild pimples, and who has ongoing lung damage. This drug was advertised on Canadian TV, in movie theatres, on billboards, and in magazines. The ads use images suggestive of use for mild acne, an unapproved use.

Elements of Precaution

Elements of Precaution: Recommendations for the Regulation of Food Biotechnology in Canada

An Expert Panel Report on the Future of Food Biotechnology prepared by The Royal Society of Canada at the request of Health Canada, the Canadian Food Inspection Agency and Environment Canada, January 2001 (*http://www.rsc.ca/ foodbiotechnology/GMreportEN.pdf*)

Following is an excerpt from this report.

THE PRECAUTIONARY PRINCIPLE AND THE REGULATION OF FOOD BIOTECHNOLOGY

INTRODUCTION

The Precautionary Principle has become a widely invoked doctrine within the field of risk regulation around the world. Though widely invoked, it is equally widely disputed and interpreted (Anon, 2000). Its roots are in the environmental movements of the 1970s, where it arose as part of a growing scepticism about the ability of scientific risk assessment and management models to predict accurately the adverse consequences of complex technologies (McIntyre and Mosedale,1997). In essence, the principle advises that, in the face of scientific uncertainty or lack of knowledge, it is better to err on the side of protecting human and environmental safety than to err on the side of the risks (i.e., "Better safe than sorry.") (Barrett, 1999).

The Precautionary Principle has been the focus of much of the debate associated with biotechnology, as with other technological developments. Its proponents view it as a proactive and anticipatory approach to technology development essential to protecting human, animal and environmental health from potentially catastrophic harms that even the best science cannot always foresee (Gullett, 1997; Barrett, 1999). Its opponents view it as an unscientific attitude that seriously inhibits economic and technological development on the basis of unfounded fears (Miller and Conko, 2000). For example, it has been suggested that the recent adoption of the principle in the Cartagena Protocol on Biosafety (see below) has the potential to "lead to arbitrary unscientific rejection of some products" (Mahoney, 2000).

CURRENT STATUS

Since its introduction in European environmental policies in the late 1970s, the Precautionary Principle has emerged as one of the principal tenets of international environmental law (Shipworth and Kenley, 1999). Today, the principle is contained in over 20 international laws, treaties, protocols and declarations (Barrett, 1999), including the Protection of the North Sea (1984), the Montreal Protocol (1997), The Bangkok Declaration on Environmentally Sound and Sustainable Development in Asia (1990), The Climate Change Convention (1992), the Rio Declaration (1992), The European Union's Maastricht Treaty (1994), and The Fish Stocks Agreement (1995, signed by over 100 countries) (McIntyre and Mosedale, 1997; Barrett, 1999).

It has also been considered by the International Court of Justice (e.g., the case of New Zealand challenging France on nuclear tests, Hungary's challenge to the Czech Republic regarding the

Danube Dams Project, and in Ireland's case against the UK regarding the risk of radioactive material entering the marine environment [the "NIREX" case]) (McIntyre and Mosedale, 1997). While the principle is not widely accepted in US law, American courts have upheld government regulatory decisions which are "precautionary like" (Cellular Telephone Co. v. Town of Oyster Bay, 166 F.3d 490, 494 (2d Cir. 1999) (Foster et al., 2000).

The Precautionary Principle has also been enshrined in international agreements affecting the regulation of plant and animal biotechnology in trade. For example, the principle is included in the Cartagena Protocol on Biosafety (agreed to in Montreal, January 2000). The treaty allows countries to use the Precautionary Principle to refuse import of GE food products. Article 11.8 states:

"Lack of scientific certainty due to insufficient relevant scientific information and knowledge regarding the extent of the potential adverse effects of a living modified organism on the conservation and sustainable use of biological diversity in the Party of import, taking also into account risks to human health, shall not prevent that Party from taking a decision, as appropriate, with regard to the import of that living modified organism intended for direct use as food or feed, or for processing, in order to avoid or minimize such potential adverse effects."

However, because the treaty later states that a rejection must be based on "credible scientific evidence," the exact impact of the treaty remains unclear (Helmuth, 2000). This proviso reflects a central unresolved issue in national and international invocations of the principle – namely, the issue of what level of scientific evidence of potential harm is required to trigger the application of precaution.

The 1992 United Nations Conference on Environment and Development (The Rio Declaration) adopted language similar to the Cartagena Protocol. Principle 15 states that "Where there are threats of serious or irreversible damage, lack of full scientific certainty shall not be used as a reason for postponing cost-effective measures to prevent environmental degradation." The Rio and Cartagena formulations are widely cited as definitive statements of the Precautionary Principle by both supporters and critics.

CONTROVERSIES SURROUNDING THE PRECAUTIONARY PRINCIPLE

As noted above, the Precautionary Principle has been the subject of much debate. Despite a substantial amount of political support throughout the world, the principle has attracted much criticism. Some of the more commonly heard criticisms of the principle include the following:

1. The Precautionary Principle lacks a uniform interpretation (Barrett, 1999). One study found 14 different interpretations of the principle (Foster et al., 2000). Some treaties, such as that of the European Union, refer to the Principle but do not actually define it. Other international instruments, such as the Cartagena Protocol, adopt it in an ambiguous manner.

2. The Precautionary Principle marginalizes the role of scientists and can be applied in an arbitrary fashion (Chapman et al., 1998; Mahoney, 2000). This criticism is based upon the concern that the invocation of the principle usually involves the relaxation of the standards of proof normally required by the scientific community. In the face of evidence less rigorous than that required for "science-based" conclusions, decision making then invokes other, extra-scientific considerations.

3. The Precautionary Principle is used as a veiled form of trade protectionism. For example, it has been claimed that the "precautionary" decision by the European markets to ban American and Canadian beef (treated with growth hormone) had an element of protectionism (Adler, 2000; Foster et al., 2000). The essence of this criticism is that the principle is used to circumvent the fundamental rules established by trade agreements enforced by the World Trade Organization, which generally require a showing by an importing country of reliable scientific evidence that an exported product poses levels of risk not accepted in domestic products (e.g. the Sanitary and Phytosanitary Agreement adopted in the Uruguay Round of GATT). The Precautionary Principle, it is argued, inherently undermines the force of this requirement

by taking the burden of scientific proof off the importing country and/or relaxing the rigour of the scientific evidence required to allege unacceptable risk. As alleged in Criticism 2, above, extra-scientific considerations then enter into a decision that should be "science-based".

4. The use of the Precautionary Principle is a form of over-regulation that will lead to a loss of potential benefits. For example, a strong biosafety protocol that limits the use of GE crops worldwide may retard advances in agricultural productivity, which could lead to global food shortages (Adler, 2000).

The persuasiveness of the latter three criticisms are clearly all related to the problem alluded to in the first one – the lack of uniform interpretation of the Precautionary Principle. The various interpretations of the principle cited in criticism (1), above, range over a wide spectrum, involving disagreement at several levels. These include disagreements over: 1) who should bear the burden of proof – those who allege potential harm, or those who deny it, 2) what the standard of proof should be for the party who bears the burden, and 3) to what extent the costs of precautionary restraint should be taken into account.

The most stringent (maximally precautionary) interpretations of the principle place the burden of proof upon the promoters of new technologies to prove its safety (no unacceptable risk), and require a high standard of proof that such risks are not involved. They counsel restraint, even if the social or economic costs of restraint are high. Proving "no-risk" in this sense is generally considered a difficult, if not impossible, scientific task.

The most permissive (minimally precautionary) interpretations of the principle, on the other hand, place most of the burden of proof upon those who allege potential risks, while perhaps relaxing the standards of proof (this is the only "precautionary" aspect), but they insist that the social and economic costs of exercising restraint be balanced against the potential risks. They "open the door to cost-benefit analysis and discretionary judgement" (Foster et al., 2000). The formulations of the Precautionary Principle in the Rio Declaration and the Cartagena Biosafety Protocol are both examples of this kind of cost-effectiveness approach.

In between these two extremes, are formulations of the principle that do not require proof of safety, but rather counsel restraint when levels of scientific uncertainty about potential risks remain high, with the burden of proof being assigned to those who develop or stand to benefit from the technology. These more moderate formulations, however, share with the more stringent formulations, the suspicion of permitting the prospect of significant benefits to override precautionary concern about the potential risks.

INTERPRETING THE PRINCIPLE

Although there is a wide diversity in the interpretation of the Precautionary Principle, it is possible to state its fundamental tenets, and to identify the points of debate within each of these tenets.

Recognition of Scientific Uncertainty and Fallibility

As noted above, the Precautionary Principle has its roots in a sense of scepticism about the ability of science, or any system of knowledge, to understand and predict fully the function of complex biological and ecological systems. The principle is essentially a rule about how to manage risks when one does not have fully reliable knowledge about the identity, character or magnitude of those risks. It assumes that there is often the possibility of error in the assessment of risks, and the higher the potential for this error, the greater the precaution it prescribes in proceeding with actions that place certain values at risk.

Uncertainty is an endemic and unavoidable aspect of any regulatory science, especially risk assessment science (Salter, 1988; Brunk et al., 1992). There are different kinds of uncertainty (Barrett, 1999) and many reasons for them. They include, among other things, the incompleteness and fallibility of the scientific models that are used to predict events and relationships in complex systems (Funtowicz and Ravetz, 1994), the incompleteness and inconsistency of data obtainable within the constraints of time and resources that normally operate within a regulatory context, and the presence of unavoidable but controversial extra-scientific assumptions (Brunk et al., 1992). The laboratory scientist can, and must, take the time and effort to reduce these uncertainties before affirming or rejecting a scientific hypothesis. The regulatory scientist, however, often does not have the time or the resources to reduce this uncertainty.

The Precautionary Principle, however variously applied, is fundamentally a rule about how technology developers, regulators and users should handle these uncertainties when assessing and managing the associated risks. Having identified the potential for error in predicting all the outcomes, the rule identifies which of these outcomes it is most important to avoid (or protect) in the event that predictions turn out to be wrong. Is it best to have erroneously lost the potential benefits in order to avoid the potential harms, or to have erroneously suffered the harms in order to realize the benefits? The Precautionary rule tends to favour the former error.

One of the most commonly cited implications of the precautionary approach is the need to respect the distinction between "absence of evidence" and "evidence of absence" when assessing and managing technological risks. For example, the claim that "there are no known adverse health or environmental effects" associated with a particular technology can mean very different things. It can mean that rigorous and intensive scientific investigation of the potential harms that might be induced by the technology has failed to show any of those harms (and, in the best case, provided a reliable explanation why the harmful effects do not or will not occur). At the other extreme, this claim might mean simply that no studies to determine if the harmful effects occur have been carried out, in which case the claim is simply an admission of ignorance. In the first instance the claim would be "evidence of absence" (of risk); in the later instance it would be simply a veiled admission of the "absence of any evidence" relevant to the question. One simple expression of the Precautionary Principle is that it counsels restraint in proceeding with the deployment of a technology in the "absence of evidence", and requires that the greater the potential risks, the stronger and more reliable be the "evidence of their absence".

Presumption in Favour of Health and Environmental Values

The Precautionary Principle is a rule about handling uncertainty in the assessment and management of risk, and the rule recommends that the uncertainty be handled in favour of certain values – health and environmental safety – over others. Uncertainty in science produces the possibility of error in the prediction of risks and benefits. The Precautionary Principle makes the assumption that if our best predictions turn out to be in error it is better to err on the side of safety. That is to say, all other things being equal, it is better to have forgone important benefits of a technology by wrongly predicting risks of harm to health or the environment than to have experienced those serious harms by wrongly failing to predict them.

Understood in terms more familiar to scientists, the Precautionary Principle can be understood to require in general that, if an error in scientific prediction should occur, it is better that it erroneously predict an adverse effect where there is in fact none (false positive, or "Type I error"), than that it erroneously predict no such effect when in fact there is one (false negative, or "Type II error") (Shrader-Frachette, 1991; Barrett, 1999). The standards of scientific research are often understood to require just the opposite value judgment – that it is far more grievous for a scientist to commit the Type I than the Type II error. The Type I error involves making a premature claim (rejection of the null hypothesis – e.g. that a GM food poses no significantly greater risk) without ample scientific evidence. Committing the Type II error merely reflects a scientifically perspicacious withholding of judgment in the face of incomplete evidence. This is what makes the Precautionary Principle appear "anti-scientific" (Criticism 2, above) to many scientists. It would appear to ask regulatory scientists to risk committing the unscientific error of affirming risks that turn out to be much lower or non-existent (rejecting the null hypothesis when it turns out to be true).*

The rules of evidence in courts of law reflect a preference with respect to uncertainty analogous to that of science. In modern democratic societies, criminal courts favour the Type II over the Type I error. It is considered far worse to convict erroneously an innocent person of a crime than to acquit erroneously a guilty person. "Better that 10 guilty persons go unpunished than that 1 innocent person be convicted" is the well-known legal axiom. In the face of legal uncertainty ("reasonable doubt" in law), the presumption should be in favour of the null hypothesis ("not guilty").

Thus, the Precautionary Principle appears to violate the rules of presumption that govern both scientific research and criminal law. Its acceptance in the regulatory context involves the judgment that, when it comes to regulating technological risks, it is better to err on the side of wrongly assuming risk than of wrongly assuming safety. This is the basis of Criticism 4 (above) that the Precautionary Principle tends to restrict the development of new technologies, and thus to retard the enjoyment of the benefits they may promise. It prefers to avoid risks, even at the expense of lost benefits, than to take those risks in order to enjoy the benefits. This, indeed, is the central force of the tenet – that given the potential of at least certain kinds and magnitudes of harms, reasonable prudence would slow the development of technologies pending stronger assurances of their safety or the implementation of active measures to guarantee safety.

The Precautionary Principle, however, need establish only a presumption in favour of safety over the benefits of a technology. Only the most stringent interpretations of the principle would demand that avoidance of risk, no matter how slight, always take priority over the enjoyment of benefits, no matter how great. Most interpretations of the principle (Pearce, 1994; Barrett, 1999) build in some sort of "proportionality rule" (O'Riordin and Jordan, 1995), which takes into consideration the costs of exercising precaution.

The greater the opportunity costs of precaution, the more significant the potential harms and the more demanding the standards of evidence for suspecting such harms. Most proponents of the Precautionary Principle hold that the presumption in favour of safety increases to the extent that the potential harm to health and environment have characteristics such as irreversibility, irremediability or catastrophic proportions. It decreases to the extent that the harms are reversible and less probable, and the costs of precaution become excessively high.

As stated earlier, the most permissive (least precautionary) interpretations of the principle hold that the costs of exercising precaution should always be balanced against the risks – that is, that a simple risk–cost–benefit analysis should determine the levels of precaution. Such an approach would in effect negate the central point of the principle, which is to create a presumption in favour of safety, since it would insist that risks and benefits be given equal weight. Even more importantly, a pure risk-cost-benefit approach is seen by many critics as anti-precautionary. This is because the usual methods by which it is carried out have a built-in bias in favour of technological benefits, which are immediate, highly predictable and quantifiable (otherwise, the technology would have no market), and against the risk factors, which are discounted because they tend to be long term, less certain and less easily quantified (Shrader-Frechette, 1991).

Proactive versus Reactive Approaches to Health and Environmental Values

Another common feature of appeals to the Precautionary Principle is inherent in the concept of "precaution" itself. It involves a requirement that the measures one takes in the face of potential harms are proactive rather than reactive. It makes the assumption that, with respect to certain kinds of technological risks, it is better to design and deploy the technologies in ways that prevent or avoid the potential harms, or guarantees the management of these risks within limits of acceptability, than to move ahead with them on the assumption that unanticipated harms can be ameliorated with future revisions or technological "fixes". This proactive aspect of precaution entails certain norms for the development of technology, which include the responsibilities: a) to carry out the appropriate research necessary to identify potential unacceptable risks; b) to withhold deployment of technologies until levels of uncertainty respecting these risks are reduced, and reasonable confidence levels concerning acceptable levels of risk are achieved; and c) to design technologies in ways that minimize health and environmental risks.

Burden of Proof and Standards of Evidence

In most legal proceedings, the party that alleges harm or offence on the part of another must shoulder the burden of proof that such harm has occurred and that it has been caused by the accused. In the case of criminal allegations, the prosecution has the burden of proof, and the standard of proof it must meet is that the evidence must establish guilt "beyond all reasonable doubt". In civil litigation, the plaintiff has the burden of proof, but the standard of proof the plaintiff must meet is usually less demanding – there must be merely a "balance of evidence" in support of the plaintiff's allegations.

Technology proponents often argue that the legal regulation of risk should follow similar principles – a technology, too, should be considered safe until proven unsafe (Miller and Conko, 2000). If the proof of risk is to be science-based in the strongest sense, it would follow that the standards of evidence should be those of research science – normally defined in terms of a 95% confidence rule (probability of error is less than 5%). This standard of evidence is the analogue in science to the "beyond all reasonable doubt" standard of evidence in criminal law.

The Precautionary Principle challenges the assumption that the regulation of environmental and health risks should always follow the legal analogy by asking whether such an approach constitutes an irresponsible attitude toward these risks. It is reasonable to invoke the legal analogy in regulatory science only on the assumption that any and all significant risks of this type can be predicted with high confidence by scientific research, not only in theory, but in actual regulatory practice. And, of course, invoking the legal analogue in regulatory science creates a strong presumption in favour of technological benefits rather than health and environmental safety. To paraphrase the legal axiom, it implies that "it is better that 10 hazardous technologies be employed to the detriment of human and environmental health than that one safe technology be erroneously restricted".

Consequently, the invocation of the Precautionary Principle nearly always involves an appeal either to shift at least some of the burden of proof (that the technology is safe) to those who propose the technology, or to relax in some way the standards of evidence required for the suspicion of unacceptable risk. Often it involves an appeal for both. Critics of the principle often argue that it puts the burden of proof upon promoters of a technology to prove (with low margins of error) its safety, which is simply unrealistic given the scientific impossibility of proving no risk (one can reject the null hypothesis, but not prove it using a standard statistical framework). There is no need to interpret the principle in such a manner, however. Proponents of the principle argue that it is equally unreasonable to place the burden of proof upon the claim of unacceptable risk, especially if the standard of proof is the normal high confidence rule required by research science. The uncertainties endemic in regulatory science are too great for this burden to be met. Such a requirement would imply that, in a case where the weight of evidence suggested the possibility of serious risk to human, animal or environmental health but confidence in the data was substantially less than the rigorous levels required for laboratory science, there would be insufficient basis for regulatory restriction of the technology.

The Precautionary Principle can be interpreted in a manner that avoids both these extremes. It can be understood to place at least a fair share of the burden of proof upon technology proponents to show that the technology will not cause unacceptable risks to health or the environment – with standards of evidence something less than the highest levels of confidence in the conclusion of "no harm". Some proponents suggest that a better standard is the one analogous to that used in civil law – "balance of evidence". A "balance of evidence" standard, in conjunction with a burden of proof to the promoter of a technology, would mean that the promoter (i.e. the applicant for registration) would have the burden of establishing that at least the weight of evidence does not support a prima facie case of serious risk. Such an approach is much more precautionary than giving the burden of higher standards of proof to the side that alleges serious risk. But, it can be argued that it still is too lenient, since it permits the approval of technologies where there is substantial, though not preponderant, evidence that unacceptable risk exists. A more precautionary approach would invoke the simple maxim that the more serious the magnitude and nature of the potential harm to health or environment, the less demanding should be the levels of confidence (the wider the margin for error) in the assumption of risk.

If there are scientific data (even though incomplete, contested, or preliminary) – plausible scientific hypotheses or models (even though contested) – together with significant levels of uncertainty, that establish a reasonable prima facie case for the possibility of serious harm (with respect to reversibility, remediation, spatial and temporal scale, complexity and connectivity), then precautionary action is justified (Barrett, 1999; Tickner, 1999). "Precaution", as noted, does not mean paralysis; it means shifting the burden of narrowing the uncertainty range and removing the theoretical unknowns to those who wish to move forward with the technology.

Sometimes, a prima facie case of risk is established by preliminary evidence that is discounted by the scientific community. The British crisis over the link between BSE ("mad cow disease") and the human nvCJD (new variant Creuzfeld-Jacob Disease) provides an instructive example of precisely this situation.

The Report of the British BSE Inquiry (BSE Inquiry, 2000) documents the manner in which the scientists (The Southwood Working Party) advising the British Ministry of Agriculture, Fisheries and Food (MAFF) assessed the preliminary evidence that BSE posed a health risk to humans. The Southwood Report assessed the risk to humans as "remote", but nevertheless made two recommendations it considered "precautionary" – that sick cows be taken out of the food chain and that bovine offal not be used in baby food. They did not recommend any further precautionary restriction on food use of subclinically infected animals (even though the long incubation period of BSE was well known). Because of the "remoteness" of the risk, such action was not considered "reasonably practical" (BSE Inquiry, 2000, Chapter 4).[1] The BSE Inquiry Report concluded that the scientific working group's dismissal of the human health risks as "remote" was a significant factor in communicating to the government and to consumers that further precautionary measures were unnecessary. The Inquiry Report wondered why, if it was "reasonably practical" to be precautionary with respect to baby food, it is not also reasonable with respect to adult food, especially since the scientists had concluded their report with the caution that "if our assessment of these likelihoods are [sic] incorrect, the implications would be extremely serious." Unfortunately, this caution was lost sight of by scientists and regulators, and was cited "as if it demonstrated as a matter of scientific certainty, rather than provisional opinion, that any risk to humans from BSE was remote" (BSE Inquiry, 2000).

What disturbed the BSE Inquiry most was the way the British MAFF responded to the preliminary assessment of the scientific work group. The Inquiry concluded that, rather than acting in an appropriately precautionary way, by taking steps to protect the British public against the potential "extremely serious" risks, the government became "preoccupied with preventing an alarmist over-reaction to BSE because it believed that the risk was remote...The possibility of a risk to humans was not communicated to the public or to those whose job it was to implement and enforce the precautionary measures" (BSE Inquiry, 2000, Executive Summary). The implications of the BSE Inquiry Report are, therefore, clear: even when the available scientific evidence fails to establish a risk as anything other than "remote", where there is a prima facie case of serious risk, significant (in this case highly costly) precautionary action is warranted.

Because the British government did not act early enough upon the growing evidence of human health risks, public confidence in both government and science was seriously eroded. As the Inquiry Report put it, "The public felt that they had been betrayed. Confidence in government pronouncements about risk was a further casualty of BSE" (BSE Inquiry, 2000, Executive Summary). The current moratorium on GM crops in the UK is widely seen as the only politically viable response to a public that has lost confidence in the ability of science, government or industry to protect public health.

Standards of Acceptable Risk (Safety)

Finally, the Precautionary Principle involves certain assumptions about what standards of safety are appropriately applied by risk regulators to different kinds of risk. The question of whether a technology is "safe" is widely recognized as a value judgment about whether a risk exceeds some level of acceptability. The acceptability of any given risk is determined by multiple factors, among the most important of which are the degree of voluntary choice involved in the risk taking, the off-setting benefits of the risk taking (and the fair distribution of the risks and benefits), the familiarity of the risk and the perceived ability to control it, the trustworthiness of the risk manager, and a whole range of highly subjective attitudes and fears associated with particular groups in particular circumstances (Fischhoff et al., 1981).

It is well known that risks associated with potentially catastrophic events (i.e., events involving dreaded harms occurring at high orders of magnitude, which are unforeseen and/or uncontrollable, and which may be irremediable) have extremely low levels of acceptability in public consciousness. When hazard magnitudes are catastrophic in nature, even extremely low probabilities of occurrence are often not sufficient to render the risk acceptable. These are the scenarios that typically invoke public demands for "zero-risk".[2] Other safety standards commonly invoked in the context of health risks in food (e.g. chemical residues, microbiological risks, artificial additives) include "threshold" standards (those that set levels of acceptability at certain specified limits) such as NOAEL ("No Observable Adverse Effect Level) and "No Higher than Background Levels".

In cases where risks and benefits tend to be evenly distributed among risk stakeholders (those who bear the risks also enjoy the benefits), so-called "balancing" standards such as risk-cost-benefit and cost-effectiveness standards tend to be more appropriate. In Chapter 7, we identified a critical ambivalence in the concept of "substantial equivalence" as it is invoked in the regulatory environment of many countries and in international standards. We have expressed serious concerns about its use as a decision threshold for exempting new genetically engineered products from rigorous safety assessment, which, as noted above, may not always be consistent with a duly precautionary approach.

However, the concept also often serves a different function – that of establishing a standard by which a GM product can be considered safe for human and animal health and for the environment. Used in this way, it functions primarily as a "No Higher than Background Level" threshold safety standard. It sets a benchmark of risk acceptability, requiring that the health and environmental risks of GM products be no higher than those associated with their non-GM counterparts. It is based upon the assumption, not that traditional native and hybridized plants are entirely free of risks, but that whatever these risks may be, they are part of the normal background of risk that society has come to view as acceptable. If the employment of a new, GM food can be shown (not assumed) to be "substantially equivalent" in the types and magnitudes of health or environmental risks to those posed by the employment of its traditional, non-GM alternative, by this standard it, too, should be considered acceptable or "safe". Understood and applied in this way, "substantial equivalence" would appear to be a fairly rigorous precautionary safety standard. Consistently applied, it would question the safety of any GM food for which there was evidence of risks higher than those known to be posed by its traditional counterpart. It represents a more precautionary standard than the "balancing" standards (e.g. ALARA, Cost-Effectiveness, Risk-Cost-Benefit) typically employed by risk managers and regulators. These latter standards are all willing to "trade off" significant risks in order to limit the costs of safety or to realize certain economic and other benefits.

IMPLICATIONS FOR THE REGULATION OF FOOD BIOTECHNOLOGY

The debate over the meaning and proper application of the Precautionary Principle cannot be settled by this Expert Panel. However, because the principle has become deeply embedded inthe many international agreements and protocols to which the Canadian government is a party, and is increasingly affirmed by European, North American and international regulatory bodies as a guiding principle for policy (CFIA, 1997; Barrett, 1999), it is appropriate that Canadian biotechnology regulatory policy reflect the basic sentiments and spirit of the principle. The recommendations contained in this Report assume that the fundamental tenets of the Precautionary Principle should be respected in the management of the risks associated with food biotechnology. All of these recommendations can be implemented within the existing regulatory framework. Our approach to the issues we consider within this Report is based upon what we consider the following precautionary rules:

RECOMMENDATIONS

1. In general, those who are responsible for the regulation of new technologies should not presume its safety unless there is a reliable scientific basis for considering it safe. This approach is especially appropriate for those who are responsible for the protection of health and the environment on behalf of the Canadian people. Any regulatory mechanism which assumes that a new product is safe on less than fully scientifically substantiated basis violates this fundamental tenet of precaution. The Expert Panel rejected the use of "substantial equivalence" as a decision threshold to exempt new GM products from rigorous safety assessments on the basis of superficial similarities (Chapter 7), because such a regulatory procedure is not a precautionary assignment of the burden of proof.

2. The proponents and developers of food biotechnology products bear a serious responsibility to subject these products to the most rigorous scientific risk assessment. In this sense, the primary burden of proof is upon those who would deploy these food biotechnology products to carry out the full range of tests necessary to demonstrate reliably that they do not pose unacceptable risks. The laws and regulations under which these products are regulated and approved in Canada already place this burden or proof upon producers of these technologies insofar as they require the producers or proponents to carry out the tests and submit data from these tests demonstrating that the products are safe.

3. Where there are scientifically reasonable theoretical or empirical grounds establishing a prima facie case for the possibility of serious harms to human health, animal health or the environment, the fact that the best available test data are unable to

establish with high confidence the existence or level of the risk should not be taken as a reason for withholding regulatory restraint on the product. In such cases, regulators should impose upon applicants for approval of the technology the obligation to carry out further research which can establish on reasonable weight of evidence that unacceptable levels of risk are not imposed by the technology.

4. Serious risks to human health, such as the potential for allergens in genetically engineered foods, risks of extensive, irremediable disruptions to the natural ecosystems through emergence of highly aggressive or invasive weed species, or of serious diminution of biodiversity, demand that the best scientific methods be employed to reduce the uncertainties with respect to these risks. Approval of products with these potentially serious risks should await the reduction of scientific uncertainty to minimum levels. The Expert Panel supports the view of the British BSE Inquiry, as discussed above, in this regard. Even though the risks appeared remote on the basis of the available evidence, the potential seriousness of the health risks justified extraordinary precaution before a fuller scientific picture was available.

5. Regulatory action in accord with the Precautionary Principle means the imposition of more "conservative" safety standards with respect to certain kinds of risks. Where there are health or environmental risks involving catastrophe scenarios (e.g. the potential effects of global warming), the greater the case for more conservative safety standards such as "zero-risk" or low threshold standards, such as that of "substantial equivalence", as articulated above. In the Panel's view, when "substantial equivalence" is invoked as an unambiguous safety standard (and not as a decision threshold for risk assessment) it stipulates a reasonably conservative standard of safety consistent with a precautionary approach to the regulation of risks associated with GM foods.

REFERENCES

Adler, J. 2000. *More sorry than safe: assessing the precautionary principle and the proposed international biosafety protocol.* Tex. Int. Law J. 35: 173–205.

Anon. 2000. Harvard International Conference on Biotechnology in the Global Economy: *Science and the Precautionary Principle*, 22–23 September 2000. Sustainable Dev. 30(2).

Barrett, K.J. 1999. *Canadian Agricultural Biotechnology: Risk Assessment and the Precautionary Principle.* Ph.D. Thesis. Vancouver: University of British Columbia.

Brunk, C.G., L. Haworth, B. Lee. 1992. *Value Assumptions Is Risk Assessment. A Case Study of the Alachlor Controversy.* Waterloo, ON: Wilfrid Laurier Press.

The BSE Inquiry: The Report. 20 Nov 2000. *The Inquiry into BSE and Variant CJD in the United Kingdom.* At: <*http://www. bseinquiry.gov.uk/*>

CFIA (Canadian Food Inspection Agency). 1997. *Comments on Mad Cows and Mothers' Milk.* At: <*www.cfia-acia.agr.ca/english/ ppc/biotech/madcow.html*>

Chapman P., A. Fairbrother, D. Brown. 1998. *A critical evaluation of safety (uncertainty) factors for ecological risk assessment.* Environ. Toxicol. Chem. 17: 99–108.

Fischhoff, B., S. Lichtenstein, P. Slovic, S. Derby, R. Keeney. 1981. *Acceptable Risk.* Cambridge: Cambridge University Press.

Foster K.R., P. Vecchia, M. Repacholi. 2000. *Science and the precautionary principle.* Science 288: 979–81.

Funtowicz, S.O., J.R. Ravetz. 1994. *Uncertainty and regulation.* In F. Campagnari et al. (eds.), Scientific-Technical Backgrounds for

Biotechnology Regulations. Brussels and Luxembourg: ECSC<
EEC<EAEC.

Gullet W. 1997. *Environmental protection and the "precautionary principle": a response to scientific uncertainty in environmental management.* Environ. Plann. Law J. 14: 52–69.

Helmuth L. 2000. *Both sides claim victory in trade pact.* Science 287: 782–83.

Mahoney, R. 2000. *Opportunity for agricultural biotechnology.* Science 288: 615.

McIntyre O., T. Mosedale. 1997. *The precautionary principle as a norm of customary international law.* J. Environ. Law 9: 221–41.

Miller, H., G. Conko. 2000. *Letter to the editor.* Nature Biotechnol. 18(July): 697–98.

O'Riordin T., A. Jordan, A. 1995. *The precautionary principle in contemporary environmental politics.* Environ. Values 4.

Pearce, D. 1994. *The precautionary principle and economic analysis.* In T. O'Riordin, J. Cameron (eds.), Interpreting the Precautionary Principle. London: Earthscan.

Salter, L., E. Levy, W. Leiss. 1988. *Mandated Science. Science and Scientists in the Making of Standards.* Boston: Kluwer Academic Publishers.

Shrader-Frechette, K.S. 1991. *Risk and Rationality.* Berkeley, CA: University of California Press.

Shipworth D., R. Kenley. 1999. *Fitness landscapes and the precautionary principle: the geometry of environmental risk.* Environ. Manage. 24: 121–31.

Tickner, J. 1999. *A map towards precautionary decision-making.* In C. Raffensperger, J. Tickner (eds.), Protecting Public Health and the Environment: Implementing the Precautionary Principle. Washington, DC: Island Press.

NOTES

1. The Working Group invoked the principle known as ALARP (As Low As Reasonably Practicable). It requires an exercise in proportionality. When deciding whether a precaution is "reasonably practicable," it is necessary to weigh the cost and consequences of introducing the precaution against the risk which the precaution is intended to obviate.

2. The demand for "zero risk" is often viewed by risk experts as irrational, because there is no such thing as an absolute zero risk for any possible hazard occurrence. This is, strictly speaking, true. However, the demand for "zero risk" often can be interpreted as an expression of zero tolerance for any incremental increase in the already occurring background risk. For example, in the current debate about the impact of pollen from Bt-engineered crops upon the Monarch butterfly, there is evidence that these crops may pose some risk to the Monarch. But many argue that the risk is marginal in comparison with other greater risks imposed upon the species, such as destruction of its habitat. The question here is what level of risk is acceptably imposed upon this species. The insistence by some that no risk from Bt crops to the Monarch is acceptable is not a call for "zero risk" in any absolute form, but rather a call for zero increase in the cumulative risk burden already imposed upon the species.

The Royal Society of Canada
The Canadian Academy of the Sciences and Humanities
La Société royale du Canada
L'Académie canadienne des sciences, des arts et des lettres

February 5, 2001

Ian C. Green
Deputy Minister
Health Canada
Ottawa Canada
K1A 0K9

Dear Mr. Green:

Thank you for your letter to Dr. William Leiss concerning the RSC Expert Panel and its interpretation of the use of the Substantial Equivalence concept at Health Canada. Dr. Leiss forwarded your letter to us, and asked us to respond.

We understand, both from the published documents and from interviews with Health Canada personnel, that the Health Canada safety assessment process does include some consideration of the five aspects listed in your letter. Those formal procedures are referenced in our Report (Chapter 3). We also understand that data related to DNA, RNA and protein expression derived directly from the transgene are reviewed.

However, in our direct discussions, Health Canada personnel did not provide sufficient information to allow us to assess the extent or rigour of the protocols used. Our request at the time for detailed data pertinent to those protocols produced no subsequent response. The Expert Panel was therefore unable to verify the overall consistency or appropriateness of the assessment process. It did, however, appear that examination of molecular biological data during the Health Canada assessments did not routinely extend to possible pleiotropic impacts of the transgene.

We appreciate that the basis of the approach used by Health Canada is an analysis of whether a claim of Substantial Equivalence can eventually be justified. However, that analysis is based solely on data and information provided by the petitioner, and the decision documents describing and validating the outcome are, as you point out, internal, and thus not readily available to either the scientific community or general public.

...2

This document was obtained
through Access-to-Information
by Gatineau-based researcher
Bradford Duplisea

In the view of the Expert Panel, this situation does not meet the expectations of either stakeholder group for a full, rigorous and transparent evaluation of GM crops and foods. Our Report details our concerns about the existing regulatory process, and offers constructive suggestions for ways in which the credibility and reliability of that process could be improved. We hope that the work of the Expert Panel will be of value in designing a regulatory process that will more effectively serve the needs of Canadian society.

Sincerely yours,

Conrad Brunk and Brian Ellis
Co-Chairs, RSC Expert Panel on the Future of Food Biotechnology

40 Questions for Health Canada

1   Why does Health Canada's proposal for legislative "renewal" ignore or misrepresent: a) the 1997 Krever Report into Tainted Blood; b) the 1998 public consultation on health protection renewal; c) the Minister's Science Advisory Board reports; d) the Auditor-General of Canada Reports; and e) the 2001 Royal Society of Canada Expert Panel on Food Biotechnology?

2   Why is the Minister of Health promoting a trade and industry agenda ("Smart" regulation), when his statutory duty is to protect health? If the Minister of Health won't protect health, who in the Government of Canada will?

3   How many lives are government and business élites prepared to sacrifice on the altars of *innovation*, *competitiveness*, *the knowledge-based economy*, and *biotechnology*?

4   Does "integrating market openness into the regulatory process" at Health Canada mean that trade in HIV blood from an Arkansas jail and BSE-infected animal feed from the U.K. will henceforth be considered examples of "smart" regulation?

5   Does the Minister of Health expect Canadians to believe that the proposal to *"Renew Federal Health Protection Legislation"* is the "result of lessons learned from the Krever Inquiry"? Is dropping the statutory "duty of care" one of the lessons learned?

6   Why has Health Canada failed to act on the necessary measures identified by the Auditor-General of Canada to provide an appropriate standard of care in order to save lives and reduce the risk of regulatory negligence?

7   Where is the evidence to support the statement that Justice Krever and the Auditor-General "recommended changes to the legislation under which Health Canada operates"?

8   If the recent changes to the Health Protection Branch, including the elimination of the word "protection" from the Branch's name, were designed to *strengthen* the health protection program, why did the Department's Deputy Minister refer to these changes as "the nasty core"?

9   When did the government get the mandate to shift from health protection to risk management?

10   Is the policy that puts a chemical giant like Monsanto in charge of researching and assessing the safety of its own products in total secrecy (genetically modified bovine growth hormone, potatoes and wheat) an example of "Smart Regulation"?

11   If health and safety came first at Health Canada, why were Department scientists under pressure to approve a genetically modified bovine growth hormone and then gagged and disciplined when they refused to approve the drug without data demonstrating the safety of the product as required by law?

12   If Health Canada ignored the call for the application of the Precautionary Principle from the Krever Inquiry and the Royal Society's Expert Panel Report on the Future of Food Biotechnology, is it reasonable for Canadians to assume the current consultation is being conducted in good faith?

13   If the food and chemical industries have convinced Health Canada that eating lead is not a health risk, what else are we expected to swallow?

14   Why did Health Canada apply the Precautionary Principle in regulating yo-yo's (a known and controllable risk) but refuse to use the Precautionary Principle in regulating GM food or pesticides (unknown, uncontrollable, and high risk, affecting future generations)?

15   If Health Canada's proposed legislation puts "safety first," as claimed, why is the vague principle "concept of precaution" listed third after two principles as guides that negate the use of precaution in risk decision-making, namely, "science-based risk assessment" and "cost-benefit analysis"?

16   What does the vague wording "concept of precaution will be applied" mean? If safety comes first, why is there no reference anywhere to the Precautionary Principle?

17   Why is the economic principle of cost-benefit analysis listed as a guide for safety assessment? If safety is in fact being put first, why weigh the negative effects on the powerless against the potential advantages for the economically powerful?

18   If safety and precaution come first, why are the guiding principles designed "For Risk Decision-Making," and not for preventive management of risk and risk prevention strategies?

19   How is the "Fundamental Values" section of the proposal consistent with the regulatory policy, international trade positions, and risk management framework of the central agencies of the Government of Canada, all of which put risk benefits before safety?

20   Why is Health Canada not enforcing the current provisions of the *Food & Drugs Act* requiring a manufacturer to demonstrate product safety before it is approved?

21 Why is the General Safety Requirement (GSR) – instead of the Precautionary Principle – the centrepiece of the new health protection proposal?

22 How does the public get a higher level of health protection from a lower standard of safety?

23 Why is Health Canada proposing a GSR, when a study it commissioned on the matter concluded that a GSR was not in the public interest?

24 Is the GSR Health Canada's attempt at "smart" regulation?

25 Would the adoption of the GSR, as proposed, make it illegal to manufacture or market meat infected with E-Coli (Hamburger Disease)?

26 Why does Health Canada keep secret the information upon which it bases its decision to approve a product? Why should Canadians trust a culture of secrecy that risks lives?

27 Why does Health Canada have transparency and openness in the regulatory process *for industry* (e.g., making and bending the rules, self-regulatory regimes, standards development), but resist transparency and openness *for the public* (e.g., information on the safety of products)?

28 Who is Health Canada's "client"?

29 Why is Health Canada not monitoring adverse drug reactions and keeping data on the number of injuries and deaths occurring each year in Canada as a result of medicine use and misuse?

30 What evidence does Health Canada have that a speedier drug approval process would lead to health benefits for Canadians, given the lack of evidence of therapeutic advantage for most new drugs, and the serious potential for harm when new drugs are belatedly found to have unexpected harmful effects?

31   Given the evidence from the Women's Health Initiative trial that the prescribing of hormone replacement therapy for disease prevention is likely to have led to unnecessary heart attacks, strokes, potentially fatal blood clots, breast cancer and dementia among the millions of Canadian women prescribed this therapy, and the evidence from the ALLHAT trial of unnecessary strokes and heart attacks among the millions of Canadians prescribed newer anti-hypertensives rather than more effective older therapies, why is Health Canada not changing the drug approval process to require evidence of a therapeutic advantage, in terms of true health outcomes, for new drugs?

32   Why is Health Canada aiming to speed up the drug approval process when more than 90% of new drugs do not offer any significant therapeutic benefit over existing drugs?

33   Why is Health Canada not strengthening its examination of the information submitted by drug companies in the approval process, since research has shown that, when drug companies sponsor studies, they are more than four times as likely to show positive results than when funding comes from other sources?

34   How are Canadians expected to react when they learn that Health Canada is willing to "trade off" potential adverse and irreversible effects to health and the environment in order to promote biotechnology in "novel" (GM) food and drugs?

35   When did Health Canada's policy change from health protection to promoting the "risk-benefits" of biotechnology in food and drugs? What is the legal basis for a policy that abandons the "duty of care" for health and safety?

36   Why did Health Canada ignore the Royal Society's Expert Panel Report: *Elements of Precaution* and its recommendation to immediately adopt the Precautionary Principle as the basis for regulating food biotechnology?

37 If Health Canada's approval of GM food is science-based, as it contends, where is the science?

38 When did the Canadian people or Parliament debate the benefits and risks of biotechnology in general and genetically modified food in particular?

39 Since 97% of Canadians want GM food labelled, why does Health Canada prevent mandatory labelling?

40 When all the evidence shows that direct-to-consumer advertising of drugs is not in the public interest and will have a negative impact on health policy, drug insurance plans, and public health, why is Health Canada even discussing this industry proposal?

References

RISK

Beck, Ulrich, *World Risk Society*, Cambridge, 1999.

Beck, Ulrich, "Risk Society and the Provident State," in S. Lash et al, eds, *Risk, Environment and Modernity*, London, 1996.

Brunk, Conrad, et al, *Value Assumptions In Risk Assessment: A Case Study of the Alachlor Controversy*, Waterloo, ON, 1992.

Brunk, C.G., "Issues of risk communication in public debates about health and safety: The BSE crisis", Presentation to joint WHO/FAO/OIE technical consultation on BSE, Paris, 2001.

Giddens, Anthony, *Runaway World: How Globalisation is Reshaping our Lives*, New York, 2003.

Jasanoff, Sheila, "Bridging the Two Cultures of Risk Analysis," *Risk Analysis*, Vol. 13, No. 2, 1993.

Lofstedt, Ragnar and Frewer, Lynn, ed., *The Earthscan Reader in Risk & Modern Society*, London, 1998.

O'Brien, Mary, *Making Better Environmental Decisions An Alternative to Risk Assessment*, Cambridge, MIT, 2000.

Proctor, Robert, *Cancer Wars: How Politics Shapes What We Know & Don't Know About Cancer*, New York, 1995.

Rachel's Environment & Health Weakly, "Why risk assessment is not a good method of determining safety," # 706, August 17, 2000. (*www.rachel.org*)

PRECAUTIONARY PRINCIPLE

Harremoes, Paul, et al, eds, *The Precautionary Principle in the 20th Century: Late Lessons From Early Warnings*, London, 2002.

Lee, Stuart, and Barrett, Katherine, "Comments on: A Canadian Perspective on the Precautionary Approach/Principle Discussion Document," Science and Environmental Health Network, 2002. (*www.sehn.org/canpre.htm*)

O'Riordan, Tim and Cameron, J., eds, *Re-Interpreting the Precautionary Principle*, London, 1994.

Raffensperger, Carolyn, *Protecting Public Health & the Environment: Implementing the Precautionary Principle*, Washington, 1999.

Royal Society of Canada, *Elements of Precaution: Recommendations for the Regulation of Food Biotechnology in Canada*, Ottawa, pp.194-210, 2002. (*www.rsc.ca*)

Science and Environmental Health Network, The Precautionary Principle Handbook, 1988. (*http://www.sehn.org/precaution.html*)

Science and Environmental Health Network, "Questions For Precautionary Thinking," The Networker, May 2001. (*http://www.sehn.org/Volume_7-3_1.html*)

Sterling, Andy, "The Precautionary Principle in Science and Technology", in Tim O'Riordan and J. Cameron, eds, *Re-Interpreting the Precautionary Principle*, London, 1994.

CORPORATE MANIPULATION OF CANADIAN REGULATORY POLICY

Auditor-General of Canada, "Federal Health and Safety Regulatory Programs," Chapter 24, December 2000. (*www.oag-bvg.gc.ca*)

Doern, C. Burce, ed., *Risky Business: Canada's Changing Science-Based Policy and Regulatory Regime*, Toronto, 2000.

Picard, André, *The Gift of Death: Confronting Canada's Tainted Blood Tragedy*, Toronto, 1998.

Regush, Nicholas, *Safety Last: The Failure of the Consumer Health Protection System in Canada*, Toronto, 1993.

Stewart, Lyle, "Good PR is growing: Ottawa is spending millions getting Canadians to shut up and eat their genetically modified veggies," in This Magazine, May/June 2000.

Stewart, Walter, *Dismantling the State: Downsizing to Disaster*, Toronto, 1998.

Treasury Board of Canada (*www.tbs-sct.gc.ca/pubs_pol/dcgpubs/manbetseries/VOL14-1_e.asp#appea*)

CORPORATE MANIPULATION OF SCIENCE

Clarke, Ann, "What is 'sound science'?", Plant Agriculture, University of Guelph, 2000. (*http://www.plant.uoguelph.ca/directory/faculty/faculty.htm*)

Fagin Dan, et al, *Toxic Deception: How the Chemical Industry Manipulates Science, Bends the Law, and Endangers Your Health*, Sesaucus, N.J., 1996.

Levidow, Les, and Carr, Susan, "Unsound Science? Trans-Atlantic Regulatory Dispute over GM Crops," Centre for Technology Strategy, 2000.

Rampton, Sheldon and Stauber, John, *Trust Us, We're Experts! How Industry Manipulates Science and Gambles with Your Future*, New York, 2001.

Schafer, Arthur, "Biomedical Conflicts of Interest: A defence of the sequestration thesis, learning from the cases of Nancy Olivieri and David Healy," British Medical Journal, 2003. (*http://jme.bmjjournals.com/cgi/data/28/2/DC1/12*)

Stauber, John, Rampton, Sheldon, *Toxic Sludge is Good For You! Lies, Damn Lies and the Public Relations Industry*, Monroe, Maine, 1995.

CORPORATE MANIPULATION OF FOOD REGULATION

Boseley, Sarah, "WHO 'infiltrated by food industry'," The Guardian (UK), January 9, 2003.

Nestle, Marion, *Food Politics: How the Food Industry Influences Nutrition and Health*, Berkeley, Ca., 2002.

Public Citizen, *Safeguards at Risk: John Graham and Corporate America's Back Door to the Bush White House*, Washington, 2001. (*www.citizen.org*)

Sarjeant, Doris, and Evans, Karen, *Hard to Swallow: The Truth About Food Additives*, Burnaby B.C., 1999.

Verrall, John, "The Manipulation of Codex Alimentarius," 1999. (*www.healthcoalition.ca/jv-codex.pdf*)

CORPORATE MANIPULATION OF GM FOOD & BIOTECHNOLOGY

Boyens, Ingeborg, *Unnatural Harvest: How Corporate Science is Secretly Altering Our Food*, Toronto, 1999.

Commoner, Barry, "Unraveling the DNA Myth: The spurious foundation of genetic engineering," Harper's Magazine, February 2002.

Economic & Social Research Council, "The Politics of GM Food," Sussex, UK, 1999. (*www.gecko.ac.uk*)

Food Ethics Council, "Engineering Nutrition: GM Crops for Global Justice?", Brighton, UK, 2003. (*www.foodethicscouncil.org*)

Ho, Mae-Wan, *Genetic Engineering: Dream or Nightmare? The Brave New World of Bad Science and Big Business*, Bath, UK, 1998.

Kneen, Brewster, *Farmageddon: Food and the Culture of Biotechnology*, B.C., 1999.

Laidlaw, Stuart, *Secret Ingredients: The Brave New World of Industrial Farming*, Toronto, 2003.

CORPORATE MANIPULATION OF DRUG REGULATION & RESEARCH

Abraham, John, "The pharmaceutical industry as a political player," in The Lancet, November 9, 2002. (*www.thelancet.com*)

Angell, Marcia, *The Truth About The Drug Companies: How They Deceive Us And What To Do About It*, New York, 2004.

Baird, Patricia, "Getting it right: Industry sponsorship and medical research," Canadian Medical Association Journal, May 13, 2003. (*http://www.cmaj.ca/cgi/content/full/168/10/1267*)

Canadian Association of University Teachers, *The Olivieri Report*, Toronto, 2001. (*http://www.caut.ca/english/issues/acadfreedom/Olivieri*)

Healy, David, *Let Them Eat Prozac*, Toronto, 2003. (*http://www.healyprozac.com/*)

Lexchin, Joel, "Hear No Secrets, See No Secrets, Speak No Secrets: Secrecy in the Canadian Drug Approval System," in International Journal of Health Services, Vol. 29, No. 1, 1999. (*http://baywood.com*)

Mintzes, Barbara, "How Does Direct-to-consumer advertising (DTCA) affect prescribing?", Canadian Medical Association Journal, September 2, 2003. (*http://www.cmaj.ca/cgi/reprint/169/5/405.pdf*)

Motchane, Jean-Loup, "Quand l'OMS épouse la cause des firmes pharmaceutiques", dans Le Monde Diplomatique, Juillet 2002. (*www.monde-diplomatique.fr*)

Moynihan, R., et al, "Selling sickness: the pharmaceutical industry and disease mongering," British Medical Journal, 2002; Vol. 324: 886-91.

WOMEN AND HEALTH PROTECTION

Batt, Sharon, *Patient No More: The Politics of Breast Cancer*, London, 1994.

Exposure: *The Breast Cancer Epidemic* (film) directed by Dorothy Rosenberg, Toronto, 1997.

Hawkins, Mary, *Unshielded: The Human Cost of the Dalkon Shield*, Toronto, 1997.

Potts. Laura, "Lies, Damn Lies and Public Protection: Corporate Responsibility and Breast Cancer Activism." (*www.bridgew.edu/ depts/artscnce/jiws/June01/lpotts.pdf*)

Reynolds, Ellen, "Beyond DES – Hormones in the Environment," in Centres of Excellence for Women's Health Research Bulletin, pp. 19-22, Spring 2003.

PUBLIC ACCOUNTABILITY

McCandless, Henry, *A Citizen's Guide to Public Accountability: Changing The Relationship Between Citizens and Authorities*, Victoria, 2002.

DOUBLESPEAK

Clarke, Ann, "Industry and Academic Biotechnology: Teaching Students the Art of Doublespeak," University of Guelph, 2002. (*www.plant.uoguelph.ca/directory/faculty/faculty.htm*)